W9-AAR-913

Over 200 Questions Children Ask about God and the Bible

Written by:
David R. Veerman, M.Div.
James C. Galvin, Ed.D.
James C. Wilhoit, Ph.D.
Daryl J. Lucas
Richard Osborne

Illustrated by:
Lil Crump

FAMILY CHRISTIAN PRESS

Visit Tyndale's exciting Web site at www.tyndale.com

Copyright © 1997 by Tyndale House Publishers, Inc. All rights reserved.

Illustrations by Lil Crump. "Jason and Max" © 1989 Impartation Idea, Inc. All rights reserved.

Over 200 Questions Children Ask about God and the Bible contains material from the following previously published books:

101 Questions Children Ask about God and *102 Questions Children Ask about the Bible,* produced for Tyndale House Publishers by Lightwave Publishing, Inc. and The Livingstone Corporation.

Unless otherwise stated, Scripture quotations are taken from *The Simplified Living Bible,* copyright © 1990 by KNT Charitable Trust. All rights reserved.

Scripture quotations marked KJV are taken from the *Holy Bible,* King James Version.

Scripture quotations marked NIV are taken from the *Holy Bible,* New International Version®. NIV®. Copyright © 1973, 1978, 1984 by International Bible Society. Used by permission of Zondervan Publishing House. All rights reserved.

Scripture quotations marked NRSV are taken from the New Revised Standard Version of the Bible, copyrighted, 1989 by the Division of Christian Education of the National Council of the Churches of Christ in the United States of America, and are used by permission. All rights reserved.

ISBN 0-8423-5138-8

Printed in the United States of America

01   00   99   98
5   4   3   2   1

CONTENTS

OLD TESTAMENT EVENTS AND PEOPLE

NEW TESTAMENT EVENTS AND PEOPLE

INTRODUCTION

The purpose of this book is to help you answer your children's questions about God and his Word, the Bible.

Childhood is an ideal time to develop a thirst for God, for children then will have a lifetime of discovering God's truths and applying them. But the Bible is often intimidating to children. Children can find the stories in the Bible virtually impossible to understand, considering that they think concretely, not conceptually like adults. In addition, young children think in real time; that is, they can't quickly put stories into the proper historical context. So they may wonder if the disciples had to fight dinosaurs or why they didn't just drive to Galilee.

Children love to ask questions. Most parents could spend hours telling about the continual stream of questions that flow from their children's mouths, especially the persistent "Why?"

When a child asks a question, he or she needs to be heard and taken seriously. This is especially true in the spiritual area. It would be a grave mistake for a parent to leave a child's question unanswered or to treat it as a cute distraction, regardless of how simple or humorous it might seem. Beyond being cute, the questions are sincere attempts to find answers, to learn truth. And parents who take those questions seriously and help their children find answers move them closer to God and his Word.

This book is filled with real questions; that is, they were asked by real boys and girls. Out of scores of questions, we chose over 200 to answer. The answers have been carefully thought through and crafted, not as the last, exhaustive word on the subject, but as thorough answers that young, inquiring minds can understand. Along with each answer, you will usually find related questions, key verses, and other Bible references.

This book will help you answer your children's questions about the Bible. But as you do so:

- Look for the question behind the question. For example, if a little girl asks, "Is there church in heaven?" (question 186), she may really be envisioning an eternity of singing hymns and listening to long sermons.
- Be careful about making up an answer when you don't have one and when the Bible is silent. For example, one parent answered the question "Why do angels light up and get bright?" (question 162) by saying, "Each angel has a star for a home." Doing that only pairs fiction with truth. Too often, children will lump the stories in the Bible with superstitions and fictions they've heard and later discovered to be false. Be honest with your answers. If you don't have an answer, say so. Or suggest that you look for the answer together.
- Be ready for follow-up questions. Your answer may lead to more questions. That's the mark of a good answer—it makes the child think.
- Make your answers concrete. Children think in very literal terms, so abstract concepts such as "heaven," "sovereignty," and "God's will" are difficult for them to understand until their ability to think abstractly naturally develops. Try to give simple answers to their questions, but focus

on helping the children learn to pray, read and memorize the Bible, and do what God wants.

- Always take children's questions about the Bible seriously, even when they sound funny to you. It's amazing what little eyes see and little ears hear.
- Show your child that the best place to look for answers to questions about the Bible is the Bible! If *you* go there for the answers, so will your kids.

Jesus said, "Let the little children come to me. Don't stop them. For the Kingdom of Heaven belong to such as these" (Matthew 19:14). When your child asks questions, take the time to look up the answers together. Use this book as a tool to help you know where to find those answers.

As we carefully and lovingly answer our children's questions about the Bible, we can help them gain understanding and a love for God and his Word.

CREATION

Q: WHY DID GOD CREATE THE WORLD?

1

A: God created the world and everything in it because he enjoys making things, and he wanted to be with us. God created people because he wanted to have friends, men and women, boys and girls, with whom he could share his love. He created the world for them to live in and enjoy.

KEY VERSES: *In the beginning God created the heavens and the earth. . . . Then God looked over all that he had made. It was excellent in every way. (Genesis 1:1, 31)*

RELATED VERSES: *Genesis 1:1–2:1; Psalm 19:1; Isaiah 45:7*

RELATED QUESTIONS: *Why did God rest when all he did was speak? Why did God create water when there was milk?*

NOTE TO PARENTS: *This question is a good opportunity to tell your children that God's plan involves them. God created the world and everything in it—including your children—so that he could have people to love.*

Q: HOW DID GOD CREATE THE EARTH?

2

A: Whenever we make something, like a craft, a drawing, or a sand castle, we have to start with special materials, like clay, string, glue, paper, crayons, and sand. We can't even imagine creating something out of nothing—by just saying the words and making it appear. But God is so powerful that he can do what is impossible for us. That includes making anything he wants, even creating things from nothing. That's what it means to be God—he can do anything.

KEY VERSES: *Before anything else existed, there was God's Son. He was the Word, and he was with God. He has always been alive and is himself God. He created everything there is. Nothing exists that he didn't make. (John 1:1-3)*

RELATED VERSES: *Genesis 1:1-2; Hebrews 1:10; 2 Peter 3:5-6*

RELATED QUESTIONS: *Why did it take God six days to create the world? What was everything like before God created the world?*

Q: WERE THERE DINOSAURS ON THE ARK?

3

A: Dinosaurs are popular today. They're on
television and in the comics. We even have
dinosaur stuffed toys. Scientists say that these unusual
animals lived and became extinct over a hundred
million years ago, so it's natural to wonder where they
fit into the Bible. Most Bible experts believe that
dinosaurs died out many years before the great flood
that we read about in Genesis. So there wouldn't have
been any dinosaurs around to put on the ark. Another
reason we don't read about dinosaurs in the Bible is that
the Bible wasn't written to tell us everything. It's not a
science textbook. The Bible tells us about people and
God's plan for our life.

KEY VERSES: *[God is speaking] "Look at Behemoth, which I
made just as I made you; it eats grass like an ox. Its
strength is in its loins, and its power in the muscles of its
belly. It makes its tail stiff like a cedar; the sinews of its
thighs are knit together. Its bones are tubes of bronze, its
limbs like bars of iron." (Job 40:15-19,* NRSV)

RELATED VERSES: *Genesis 7:1-24; John 1:3*

RELATED QUESTIONS: *Why don't we have dinosaurs today?
Why aren't dinosaurs mentioned in the Bible? Where do
dinosaurs fit into the Bible? Were there dinosaurs around
with Adam and Eve?*

NOTE TO PARENTS: *The Bible doesn't mention dinosaurs,
but it does say that God created everything (John 1:3).
Some verses, like the one about Behemoth, talk about
animals almost as big as dinosaurs.*

Q: WHY DID GOD MAKE MOSQUITOES?

4

A: When we're being attacked by mosquitoes, it's easy to wonder why God made pests and other animals that can harm us. When God created the world, it was perfect. Only after sin entered the picture did animals and human beings become enemies, causing humans to protect and defend themselves. So now mosquitoes try to feed off of us. They, in turn, become food for birds and bats. In the future, in the new heaven and new earth, animals won't hurt people or each other.

KEY VERSES: *In that day the wolf and the lamb will lie down together. And the leopard and goats will be at peace. Calves and fat cattle will be safe among lions. And a little child shall lead them all. The cows will graze among bears. Cubs and calves will lie down side by side. And lions will eat grass like the cows. Babies will crawl safely among deadly snakes. And a little child who puts his hand into a nest of adders will not be hurt. Nothing will hurt or destroy in all my holy mountain. And as the waters fill the sea, the earth will be full of the knowledge of the Lord. (Isaiah 11:6-9)*

RELATED VERSES: *Genesis 3:17-19; Romans 8:19-22*

RELATED QUESTIONS: *Why did God make bugs that bother us? Why did God make animals that we can't eat?*

Q: WHY DO SHARKS EAT PEOPLE?

5

A:
Sharks attack people because they are meat-eaters. When they are hungry, they will attack anything that looks good to eat. Sharks don't go looking for people to attack—they just react to what comes near them. The best thing to do is to be smart and stay away from sharks. When we go where we shouldn't go, we get into trouble—like walking in poison ivy or playing in a thunderstorm. There are dangers in the world, and we should be careful to avoid them.

KEY VERSES: *For wisdom will enter your heart, and knowledge will be pleasant to your soul. Discretion will protect you, and understanding will guard you. (Proverbs 2:10-11,* NIV)

RELATED VERSES: *Genesis 3:17-19; Numbers 21:6; Deuteronomy 32:24; Jeremiah 8:17; Ezekiel 34:25; Matthew 10:16*

RELATED QUESTIONS: *Why did God make animals that harm us? Why did God create poison ivy and poisonous plants?*

NOTE TO PARENTS: *The question of why God made animals that can harm us is answered earlier in Question 4. The answer according to Scripture is that we live in a sinful world (Genesis 3:14-19).*

Q: IF GOD MADE SPIDERS, WHY DO PEOPLE SQUISH THEM?

6

A: God created spiders just as he made all the other animals. But there's a great difference between animals and human beings. People are created in God's image and are supposed to take care of all creation—including all animals and plants. God put people in charge of creation, but this does not mean we can harm and kill for fun or destroy the world as we please. We can kill animals and plants for food and to control their population; we can remove or kill spiders, insects, and so forth that threaten us or make it difficult for us to live. But we should be kind to animals when possible and take good care of the world.

KEY VERSE: *And God blessed them and told them, "Multiply and fill the earth and subdue it. You are masters of the fish and birds and all the animals." (Genesis 1:28)*

RELATED VERSES: *Genesis 1:20-25; Proverbs 12:10; Acts 10:9-16*

NOTE TO PARENTS: *Some children want to hurt animals, while others want to be compassionate. God's desire is for us to be compassionate and wise rulers of all animal life (Proverbs 12:10). This should not be taken to such an extreme that we think eating meat is wrong. God has provided animals as a source of food and has given us permission to eat meat (see Acts 10).*

Q: WHY DID GOD MAKE PEOPLE RED AND YELLOW, BLACK AND WHITE?

7

A: Can you imagine a world in which everyone looked the same—the same height, weight, color of hair, length of nose, color of eyes, size of ears, and color of skin? That would be boring—and how would we tell people apart? Instead, God created all kinds and colors of people. Some are tall; some are short; some are brown; some are pink; some have straight black hair; some have curly red hair. They are all special to God. Don't you just love the differences and what makes you special? God does!

KEY VERSE: *In this new life your nation or race or education or social group means nothing. Christ is what matters, and he has been given to all. (Colossians 3:11)*

RELATED VERSES: *Jeremiah 13:23; Acts 17:26*

RELATED QUESTION: *How did people get different color skin when Adam and Eve were only one color?*

Q: DID GOD MAKE PEOPLE IN OUTER SPACE?

8

A: Although people may talk about creatures in outer space, no one really knows whether there is life on other planets. Most of the talk about other life forms comes from make-believe movies and what people imagine *might* be true. But if there is life in other parts of the universe, God is in charge of it because God is in charge of the whole universe. God created *everything*, and he is the God of all life everywhere, no matter where it may be.

KEY VERSE: *Christ created everything in Heaven and earth. He created the things we can see and the things we can't see. All kings and kingdoms, rulers and powers were made by Christ. He made them for his own use and glory. (Colossians 1:16)*

RELATED VERSES: *Genesis 1:1; 1 Chronicles 29:11-12*

RELATED QUESTIONS: *Are there aliens in outer space? Why did God make Mars and Jupiter?*

Q: HOW DOES GOD MAKE THE SUN AND MOON GO UP AND DOWN?

9

A: God made powerful laws to govern the universe. These laws control the movements of the sun, moon, earth, and other planets and stars. For example, one law called "gravity" draws objects toward each other. Other natural laws control the weather. Many forces determine whether the day will be sunny or cloudy, warm or cold, such as the heat from the sun, the currents in the ocean, the wind, and many others. God set up the rules that make all these forces work together. And because God controls the entire universe, he can interrupt the laws if he wants to—bring rain to dry land or bright sunshine to flooded areas. How powerful God must be to control all that!

KEY VERSE: *The heavens are telling the glory of God. They are a great display of what God can do. (Psalm 19:1)*

RELATED VERSES: *Joshua 10:13; 1 Kings 18:1ff.; 2 Kings 20:8-11; 2 Chronicles 7:12ff.; Psalm 19:1-6; 104:19; 148:3; Hebrews 1:2-3*

RELATED QUESTIONS: *How does God make the weather? Can God make the weather so that it'll be sunny tomorrow?*

NOTE TO PARENTS: *Part of this is a science issue. If your children are wondering how the forces of nature work, don't be afraid of encouraging them to learn more about the natural sciences. The power and wonder of nature can be used to inspire awe and worship of God. The heavens declare his glory! (See Psalm 19.)*

ADAM
AND
EVE

Q: WHY DID GOD MAKE PEOPLE?

10

A: People are special creations, not just different animals. God created people to be his friends and to take care of the world. Unlike animals, human beings can talk to each other and to God. People are the only part of God's marvelous creation that can be friends with God. And he created them perfect—that's why Adam and Eve were not ashamed of their nakedness. But people are also the only ones who can sin.

KEY VERSES: *Then God said, "Let us make a man—someone like ourselves. He will be the master of all life upon the earth and in the skies and in the seas." So God made man like his Maker. Like God did God make man. Man and maid did he make them. (Genesis 1:26-27)*

RELATED VERSES: *Genesis 2:4-7; Psalm 8:4-5; 139:13-18*

RELATED QUESTIONS: *Why did God make people in addition to animals? Why did God make women?*

Q: HOW DID GOD MAKE ADAM AND EVE?

11

A: God made Adam and Eve, the first human beings, by using material that he had already made. God formed Adam just the way he wanted him to look and then brought Adam to life. God made Eve from part of Adam so that she would match him perfectly.

KEY VERSES: *The time came when the Lord God formed a man's body. He made it from the dust of the ground. Then he breathed into it the breath of life. And man became a living person. . . . Then the Lord God caused the man to fall into a deep sleep. He took one of the man's ribs. Then he closed up the place from which he had taken it. Then he made the rib into a woman, and brought her to the man. (Genesis 2:7, 21-22)*

RELATED VERSES: *Genesis 1:26–2:25; 3:19; 1 Timothy 2:13*

RELATED QUESTIONS: *Why did God make Eve from Adam's rib? Why did God make us out of dust?*

NOTE TO PARENTS: *A young child's concrete understanding can be a barrier to understanding this because the creation of Adam and Eve was a miracle. Explaining it as such may be the best approach, especially if your child is asking about the exact process that God used.*

Q: WHAT DID ADAM AND EVE "DRESS" THE LAND WITH?

12

A: The word *dress* that is used in some Bible versions means "take care of" or "tend." So when God told Adam and Eve to "dress" the land, he was telling them to take care of the rest of his creation.

KEY VERSE: *And the Lord God took the man, and put him into the garden of Eden to dress it and to keep it. (Genesis 2:15,* KJV)

RELATED VERSES: *Genesis 18:7; Deuteronomy 28:39; 2 Samuel 12:4*

NOTE TO PARENTS: *This kind of question is a good example of why it is important to choose an age-appropriate translation of the Bible for your child. There are many excellent translations from which to choose. The best one for your child is the one that uses words that he or she already knows.*

Q: HOW DID GOD MAKE EVERYONE ELSE AFTER ADAM AND EVE?

13

A: When God created animals and plants, he gave them the ability to reproduce themselves. The same is true with Adam and Eve—God created them with the ability to make babies. Adam and Eve had babies; then, when those children grew up, they got married and also had children. Those children also grew up and had babies. As time went on, there were more and more people on the earth. And although God didn't make each person the same way he created Adam and Eve, he was still involved with the creation of each one, watching over and putting him or her (and you) together just right.

KEY VERSE: *Then Adam lay with Eve his wife. She conceived and gave birth to a son, Cain (meaning "I have created"). For, as she said, "With God's help, I have created a man!" Her next child was his brother, Abel. Abel became a shepherd. Cain was a farmer. (Genesis 4:1-2)*

RELATED VERSES: *Genesis 1:28; 5:1-18; 6:1; Psalm 139: 13-18; Ezekiel 36:11; Hebrews 6:14*

RELATED QUESTIONS: *Did God make me the same way he made Adam? Did Eve have a belly button?*

NOTE TO PARENTS: *Many parents avoid this issue because they are uncomfortable talking about sex. Don't communicate nonverbally that this is a dirty or embarrassing topic. But at the same time, don't give children more information than they want or need.*

Q: HOW DID ADAM KNOW WHAT TO NAME THE ANIMALS?

14

A: God gave Adam the job of naming the animals, much like when your parents might ask you to name your pet. Adam named the animals whatever he wanted. But Adam didn't speak English, so the names he used are not the ones we use today. Adam lived a very long time ago, and today each language has its own words for the animals in our world.

KEY VERSES: *So the Lord God formed from the soil every kind of animal and bird. He brought them to the man to see what he would call them. Whatever the man called them, that was their name. (Genesis 2:19-20)*

RELATED VERSES: *Acts 13:2; Colossians 4:17*

Q: WHY DID ADAM AND EVE EAT THE FORBIDDEN FRUIT IF GOD SAID NOT TO?

15

A: Adam and Eve were sinless and perfect when God created them. But they still could choose to do what was wrong (just like you can choose to do what you aren't supposed to). When the devil tempted them to eat the forbidden fruit, they chose to do it. Although people talk about Adam and Eve eating an "apple" in the Garden of Eden, we don't know what the fruit looked like or how it tasted. All we know is that it was the one fruit in that big, beautiful garden that they weren't supposed to eat. Adam and Eve ate the fruit because the devil started them thinking about what it would be like. Then he lied about God's rule to make them think that God was keeping something good from them. Pretty soon they wanted to eat the fruit more than they wanted to obey God's rule.

KEY VERSES: *The serpent was the craftiest of all the creatures the Lord God had made. So the serpent came to the woman. "Really?" he asked. "None of the fruit in the garden? God says you mustn't eat any of it?" "Of course we may eat it," the woman told him. "It's only the fruit from the tree at the center of the garden that we must not eat. God says we must not eat it or even touch it. If we do, we will die." "That's a lie" the serpent hissed. "You'll not die! God knows very well that as soon as you eat it you will become like him. Your eyes will be opened. You will be able to know good from evil!" The woman was convinced. How lovely and fresh-looking it was! And it would make her so wise! So she ate some of the fruit and gave some to her husband. He ate it too. (Genesis 3:1-6)*

RELATED VERSES: *Matthew 6:13; 26:41*

Q: WHY DIDN'T ADAM DIE WHEN GOD SAID HE WOULD?

16

A: When Adam and Eve disobeyed God and ate the fruit, sin entered the world. That was the first sin ever! And when sin came into the world, death came with it. There are two kinds of death, and both came to Adam and Eve and to the world. First, there is physical death. Although Adam and Eve didn't die immediately when they took a bite of the fruit, eventually they *would* die. From that moment on, all plants, animals, and humans would die eventually. Second, there is spiritual death. That means being separated from God, being his enemies instead of his friends. This death came to Adam and Eve, and to all of us, the moment they disobeyed God. The only way to avoid this death forever is to trust in Christ. That's why Jesus came to earth—to die in our place, for our sin, so that we might have eternal life!

KEY VERSES: *When Adam sinned, sin entered the whole human race. His sin spread death through all the world. Everything began to grow old and die because all sinned. . . . For this one man, Adam, brought death to many through his sin. But this one man, Jesus Christ, brought forgiveness to many through God's mercy. Adam's one sin brought the penalty of death to many. But Christ freely takes away many sins and gives new life instead. (Romans 5:12, 15-16)*

RELATED VERSES: *Hebrews 9:27; James 4:14*

Q: DID GOD KNOW ADAM AND EVE WERE GOING TO SIN?

17

A: God knows everything, even before it happens, so he knew that Adam and Eve were going to sin. Still, God was very disappointed with what Adam and Eve did. But because God loved them (and because he loves us), he made a way for the sin to be forgiven. God's plan was to send Jesus to die on the cross for Adam's, Eve's, and our sins. By trusting in Christ, we can have eternal life.

KEY VERSES: *Long ago, before he made the world, God chose us to be his very own. He did this because of what Christ would do for us. He decided then to make us holy in his eyes, without a single fault. We stand before him covered with his love. His plan has always been to adopt us into his own family. He would do this by sending Jesus Christ to die for us. And he did this because he wanted to! (Ephesians 1:4-5)*

RELATED VERSES: *John 2:23-25; Acts 17:26-27*

NOTE TO PARENTS: *The knowledge that God knows everything can give your children a sense of security. Children can't do anything that will surprise God. He may be happy or disappointed, but he won't be surprised. Also, be aware that your children may not understand what the word penalty means. So be prepared to offer a simple explanation.*

GOD

Q: WHAT DOES GOD LOOK LIKE?

18

A: No one knows what God "looks like" because God is invisible and doesn't have a physical body as we do. But we can learn about God and see what God acts like by learning about his Son, Jesus. In the Bible we can read about how Jesus lived, how he treated people, and what he taught. That's what God is like.

KEY VERSE: *Jesus replied, "Don't you even yet know who I am, Philip? And I have been with you for all this time! Anyone who has seen me has seen the Father! So why are you asking to see him?" (John 14:9)*

RELATED VERSES: *John 1:18; 5:37; 6:46; 1 John 3:2*

RELATED QUESTIONS: *Does God have a beard? Is God bald?*

Q: DOES GOD HAVE FRIENDS OR IS HE ALONE?

19

A: God doesn't have other "gods" to be friends with. He is the only God there is. God doesn't need friends the way we do; he is perfectly happy being alone. But God also wants to have friendship with us. In fact, God wants to be our closest friend. So he has done a lot to make friends with us and to have our friendship. That's why he created us, sent Jesus to save us, gave us the Bible, and gave us the church.

KEY VERSES: *And you are my friends if you obey me. I no longer call you slaves. For a master doesn't confide in his slaves. Now you are my friends. This is proved by the fact that I have told you all that the Father told me. (John 15:14-15)*

RELATED VERSES: *Genesis 1:26; John 17:3*

RELATED QUESTIONS: *Are there other gods? Does God ever get lonely?*

Q: WHERE DOES GOD LIVE?

20

A: Sometimes we think of God as though he were another person like us. And just as we can only be one place at a time and we need a place to live, we think that God is the same way. But God isn't limited to a physical body or to one place at a time. In fact, God lives everywhere, especially inside people who love him. We call church "God's house" because that's where people who love God gather together to worship him. But no matter where we are, God is with us. We can never be lost to his love. God also lives in heaven—eventually, we will live there, too.

KEY VERSES: *[Solomon is speaking] "But is it possible that God would live on earth? Why, even the skies and the highest heavens cannot hold you! This Temple I have built will not be able to hold you either! And yet, O Lord my God, you have heard and answered what I asked. Please watch over this Temple night and day. For this is the place you have promised to live. Please listen to my prayers here, whether by night or by day. Listen to every prayer of the people of Israel. Listen to them when they face this place to pray. Yes, hear in heaven where you live. And when you hear, forgive." (1 Kings 8:27-30)*

RELATED VERSES: *Psalm 139:7-12; Acts 17:24-29; Romans 8:38-39; Ephesians 4:8-10*

RELATED QUESTIONS: *Does God live in the mountains? Where is heaven? How can God live in my heart? Does God live in church? How can God be everywhere? Is God a person or a ghost? How big is God?*

Q: DOES GOD SLEEP, OR DOES HE JUST REST?

21

A: God does not have a physical body like us, so he doesn't need to sleep or eat. When the Bible says God "rests," it means he has stopped doing something. To us, that is like rest. But God doesn't get tired or worn out, so he doesn't need to rest the way we do. And when we go to sleep at night, God doesn't close his eyes too—he continues to watch over us.

KEY VERSES: *He will never let me stumble, slip, or fall. For he is always watching, never sleeping. (Psalm 121:3-4)*

RELATED VERSES: *Genesis 2:2; 1 Kings 18:27; Ecclesiastes 8:16-17*

RELATED QUESTIONS: *Will I be safe at night? What does God do in heaven? Does God eat?*

NOTE TO PARENTS: *This kind of question arises from the faulty thinking that God is just like people. Most false gods that have been made up by various cultures, such as those the Canaanites worshiped or the Greek gods, were much like comic book superheros—just like people with superhuman abilities. But God isn't just a greater human. Clearing up this question will correct this faulty way of thinking about God.*

Q: WHO CREATED GOD?

22

A: No one created God—he has always existed. We can't understand this because everything that we know has a beginning or an end. Each day has a morning and night; basketball games have an opening tip-off and a final buzzer; people are born and they die. But God has no beginning or end. He always was and always will be.

KEY VERSES: *Lord, through all the generations you have been our home! You were there before the mountains were made. You were there before the earth was formed. You are God without beginning or end. (Psalm 90:1-2)*

RELATED VERSES: *Hebrews 13:8; Revelation 1:8, 18*

RELATED QUESTIONS: *Where did God come from? Will God ever die? How old is God?*

Q: WHY CAN'T WE SEE GOD?

23

A: We can't see God because he's invisible. But we *can* see what he does. Balloons are filled with air that we can't see, but we see the balloon get big as the air is put in. Radio waves are invisible, but they exist. Just because we can't see God doesn't mean he isn't real. Believing that God is there even though we can't see him is *faith*. Someday, in heaven, we will see God face to face.

KEY VERSE: *We can see and understand only a little about God now. It is like we were looking at his reflection in a poor mirror. Someday we are going to see him face to face. Now all that I know is hazy and blurred. But then I will see everything clearly. I will see as clearly as God sees into my heart right now. (1 Corinthians 13:12)*

RELATED VERSES: *John 1:18; Colossians 1:15; 1 Timothy 1:17; Hebrews 11:27*

RELATED QUESTION: *Why doesn't God let everyone see him so everyone will believe him?*

NOTE TO PARENTS: *Young children struggle with this because of their concrete way of thinking. Using illustrations like the ones here are helpful, but still imperfect; we can't see air because it's molecules don't form a solid enough image for us to see, not because it has no physical form. In contrast, God is invisible to us because he is a spirit.*

Q: CAN CHRISTIANS HEAR GOD TALKING TO THEM?

24

A: In the Bible we read about people hearing God's voice. Today, the main way that God speaks to us is through the Bible. That's why it's called "God's Word"—the Bible is God's message to us. God may also speak to us through people and circumstances and in other ways. But God will never tell us to do something that goes against what he says in the Bible. And don't forget, God is with us all the time.

KEY VERSES: *Long ago God spoke in many different ways to our fathers. He spoke through the prophets in visions, dreams, and even face to face. Little by little he told them about his plans. But now in these days he has spoken to us through his Son. He has given his Son everything. Through his Son he made the world and everything there is. (Hebrews 1:1-2)*

RELATED VERSES: *1 Samuel 3:1-18; Psalm 119:1-24*

RELATED QUESTIONS: *How can I hear God? Does my heart have ears?*

Q: DAD, WHY DO I NEED TWO FATHERS, YOU AND GOD?

25

A: We call God "our Father" because he created us, watches over us, and provides everything we need. He's like a human father, only perfect. God has given us human fathers and mothers to take care of us on earth. That's why God tells children to obey their parents and their heavenly Father—it's for their own good.

KEY VERSE: *[Jesus is speaking] "You sinful men even know how to give good gifts to your children. So won't your Father in Heaven be sure to give good gifts to those who ask him for them?" (Matthew 7:11)*

RELATED VERSES: *Exodus 20:12; Ephesians 6:1-3*

RELATED QUESTIONS: *What does it mean that God is our Father? What's the same and different about human fathers and God? Why does God say kids have to obey their parents?*

Q: DOES GOD SEE EVERYTHING THAT WE DO?

26

A: Yes, God sees everything we do, both good and bad. We can't hide from him. God is happy when we do what is right and sad when we do wrong. God can reward us for doing what's right, even when no one else knows about it.

KEY VERSES: *[Elihu is speaking] "For God watches the deeds of all mankind. He sees them all. No darkness is thick enough to hide evil men from his eyes." (Job 34:21-22)*

RELATED VERSES: *Job 11:11; 31:4; Psalm 147:5; Matthew 10:28-31*

RELATED QUESTIONS: *Does God see the bad things I do? How can God know everything? How can God see everywhere?*

NOTE TO PARENTS: *This question may arise from a guilty conscience. Your child may want to talk about something that he or she did.*

JESUS

Q: IS JESUS GOD?

27

A: Jesus is fully God. When he came to earth and was born of the Virgin Mary, Jesus also became a human being, a person like you. So Jesus is both God and man. As God, Jesus has always existed—he was not created when he was born. Instead, he willingly chose to take on a human body.

KEY VERSES: *Before anything else existed, there was God's Son. He was the Word, and he was with God. He has always been alive and is himself God. (John 1:1-2)*

RELATED VERSES: *John 1:14; 14:9; Colossians 1:15-18*

RELATED QUESTION: *Did God create Jesus?*

Q: HOW CAN GOD BE THREE PERSONS AND ONE PERSON AT THE SAME TIME?

28

A: We don't know *how* God can be three persons at the same time, but we know he is because the Bible tells us so. The idea of three in one (the Trinity) is very hard to understand. Some people use the example of water. Water can be a liquid, a gas, or a solid. We usually see water in liquid form, as when we use it for drinking or for taking a bath. But water can also be a gas, as when it turns to steam. And it can be a solid, in the form of ice. But whether liquid, gas, or solid, it's still water. In some ways God is like a family with father, mother, and child—three persons and one family. Just remember that the Trinity does not mean that we have three gods. There is one God with three persons. The Trinity also does not mean that God wears three hats, or takes on three roles, at different times. All three persons—Father, Son, and Holy Spirit—have always existed.

KEY VERSE: *[Jesus is speaking] "So now go and make disciples in all the nations. Baptize them into the name of the Father, the Son, and the Holy Spirit." (Matthew 28:19)*

RELATED VERSES: *Matthew 3:16-17; John 14:7, 9-10*

RELATED QUESTION: *Why are there three people in the Trinity?*

Q: DO GOD AND JESUS CRY?

29

A: As a man, Jesus cried real tears when he was sad. God does not shed tears today, but he feels sad when people are hurting, when they disobey him, and when they don't believe in him. We can bring God joy by living as we should, showing love to others, and telling people about Christ.

KEY VERSE: *Tears came to Jesus' eyes. (John 11:35)*

RELATED VERSES: *Luke 19:41; John 11:33; Ephesians 4:30; Revelation 7:17*

RELATED QUESTION: *Does God have a heart?*

Q: **DID JESUS REALLY LIVE JUST LIKE ME, OR WAS HE PRETEND?**

30

A: Jesus is real. He came to earth and was born as a baby (we celebrate Jesus' birth at Christmas). And he lived like other ordinary people. Some stories we read and hear are made up and weren't meant to be taken as true. But the stories in the Bible really happened, and that's where we can read about Jesus.

KEY VERSE: *Christ was alive when the world began. I have seen him with my own eyes and listened to him speak. I have touched him with my own hands. He is God's message of life. (1 John 1:1)*

RELATED VERSES: *John 20:27; 1 Timothy 3:16; Hebrews 4:15*

Q: DID JESUS EVER DO ANYTHING BAD WHEN HE WAS LITTLE?

31

A: Jesus was born as a baby and grew up as a little boy and into a young man. When he was a child, Jesus had to learn many things, like how to hold a cup, how to talk, and how to count. He learned things from his parents and went to school to learn, too. But though Jesus was a real human being, he never did anything wrong—he never sinned—like stealing, lying, disobeying his parents, or saying bad words. Sometimes Jesus did things that *others* said were bad—like helping certain people and speaking out against wrong. But Jesus always did what was right—he always obeyed God.

KEY VERSES: *This suffering is all part of the work God has given you. Christ, who suffered for you, is your example. Follow in his steps. He never sinned. He never told a lie. He never answered back when insulted. When he suffered he did not threaten to get even. He left his case in the hands of God who always judges fairly. (1 Peter 2:21-23)*

RELATED VERSES: *Luke 2:41-51; Hebrews 5:9; 1 Peter 1:18-19*

RELATED QUESTIONS: *Did Jesus ever fight with his brothers? Did Jesus go to school?*

Q: IF JESUS DIED ON THE CROSS, HOW CAN HE BE ALIVE TODAY?

32

A: Jesus lived as a real human being. Jesus' death was a real death, too (he really died on the cross)—the people who killed him made sure of that. When Jesus was killed, all of his followers were very sad. Jesus' body was put in a grave. But three days later, God brought Jesus back to life. Jesus showed his wounds to his disciples. Jesus lives in his special "glorified" body in heaven today. Isn't that great?

KEY VERSES: *I passed on to you from the first what had been told to me. Christ died for our sins just as the Bible said he would. He was buried, and three days later he rose from the grave. This happened just as the prophets said it would. (1 Corinthians 15:3-4)*

RELATED VERSES: *John 20:27; 1 Corinthians 15:12-58*

RELATED QUESTIONS: *Did Jesus really die? Does Jesus still have scrapes and cuts on his body? How did Jesus rise from the dead? Is Jesus invisible now?*

NOTE TO PARENTS: *We call Jesus' postresurrection body a "glorified" body. Jesus was recognized by the disciples, and he ate a meal with them. But he also was able to appear suddenly in their midst—he wasn't limited by space and time. We really don't know anything more about what his body was like or what our body will be like. (See Luke 24:36-43 and John 20:19-31.)*

Q: WHY DO I FEEL AFRAID IF JESUS IS WITH ME?

33

A: Jesus is always with us even though we don't see him and often we don't feel any different. Jesus wants us to learn to trust him, to believe and know that he is there. It's natural to feel afraid. In fact, being afraid can be good. We should be afraid of danger. For example, fear can keep us a safe distance from a mean dog or something else that might hurt us. God wants our fears to remind us to trust him. Being afraid should be a signal to trust God and do what he wants us to do. But it doesn't mean that Jesus isn't with us.

KEY VERSE: *May the Lord of peace himself give you his peace no matter what happens. The Lord be with you all. (2 Thessalonians 3:16)*

RELATED VERSES: *Matthew 28:20; Philippians 4:6*

Q: HOW DID JESUS WALK ON WATER?

34

A: Jesus did a lot of miracles. We don't know how he did them. Jesus is God, so he can do anything. Walking on the water was not Jesus' ordinary way of getting around. He did this miracle, like other miracles, to teach his disciples and to show them his power. Jesus is Lord of the laws of the universe—he's in charge of the water, too, so he can walk on it whenever he wants to.

KEY VERSES: *That evening his disciples went down to the shore to wait for him. Darkness fell and Jesus still hadn't come back. So they got into the boat and headed out across the lake toward Capernaum. But soon a storm swept down upon them as they rowed. The sea grew very rough. And they were in the middle of the lake. Suddenly they saw Jesus walking toward the boat! They were terrified. So he called out to them and told them not to be afraid. Then they were willing to let him come to them. And suddenly the boat was already at the place where they were going! (John 6:16-21)*

RELATED VERSES: *Matthew 14:23-32; Mark 4:35-41; 6:45-51*

NOTE TO PARENTS: *Lots of well-meaning people have tried to explain miracles (such as Jesus' walking on the water) to make them believable to children. But this is a tragic mistake. The fact that miracles are incredible is exactly the point—they show us that God is awesome and powerful.*

Q: WHY DID JESUS DRESS SO FUNNY?

35

A: The clothes worn by Jesus and his followers may look different to us today, but they were in style back then. Jesus wore what people wore at that time. His clothes fit the climate and culture of the day. No one who lived in Jesus' time told him that he dressed funny, and they should know.

KEY VERSES: *So the soldiers crucified Jesus. Then they put his clothes into four piles. There was one piece of clothing for each of them. But they said, "Let's not tear up his robe," for it was seamless. "Let's throw dice to see who gets it." This fulfilled the Scriptures. It said, "They divided my clothes among them and cast lots for my robe." (John 19:23-24)*

RELATED VERSES: *Psalm 22:18; Matthew 27:35*

NOTE TO PARENTS: *Children get their idea of how Jesus dressed from Bible and Sunday school art. This is what we think Jesus might have looked like, but we have no pictures or descriptions of his physical appearance, so we don't know exactly what he looked like.*

Q: WHY DID THEY BEAT UP JESUS?

36

A: Some people got very angry at Jesus because he was speaking against the bad things they were doing. They tried to get Jesus to do what they wanted. Instead, Jesus did what God wanted him to do, and he told everybody how bad those people were. Finally the people got so angry at Jesus that they wanted to kill him. And eventually, that's what they did.

KEY VERSES: *Then the Roman soldiers took him into the barracks of the palace. They called out the whole palace guard. They dressed him in a purple robe. And they made a crown of sharp thorns and put it on his head. Then they cheered, yelling, "Yea! King of the Jews!" They beat him on the head with a cane and spat on him. They made fun of him by bowing down to "worship" him. (Mark 15:16-19)*

RELATED VERSES: *Isaiah 53:4-10; Matthew 26:57-68; Mark 15:15; John 15:14-18*

RELATED QUESTIONS: *Why did they put a thorny crown on Jesus? If Jesus was such a good man, why were people mad at him?*

Q: WHY DID GOD LET THEM HURT JESUS?

37

A: When Jesus was being hurt, he could have called on angels to save him. After all, he was God's Son. But Jesus chose to suffer and die *for us*. Jesus loved us so much that he did what it took to pay for our sins. Jesus and the Father agreed that it was necessary for him to die on the cross.

KEY VERSES: *He has so much kindness! He took away all our sins through the blood of his Son. This saved us. He has showered upon us the richness of his grace. He understands us and knows what is best for us at all times. God has told us his secret reason for sending Christ. He has a plan he decided on in mercy long ago. He plans to gather us all together when the time is ripe. He will gather his people in Heaven and on earth. They will be with him in Christ forever. (Ephesians 1:7-10)*

RELATED VERSES: *Matthew 26:53; 27:46; 1 John 2:2*

RELATED QUESTION: *Why didn't Jesus save himself from dying on the cross?*

Q: WHY DO THEY CALL IT GOOD FRIDAY IF THAT'S THE DAY JESUS DIED?

38

A: The day Jesus died is called "Good Friday" because it was a good day for us—Jesus died for us, in our place. That day was both a happy day and a sad day. It was sad because Jesus suffered and died. But it was happy because Jesus paid the penalty for our sins. At the time, the day was not seen as Good Friday. But by Easter morning, after Jesus had been raised from the dead, everybody knew it was good.

KEY VERSES: *He was taken out of the city. He carried his cross to the place known as "The Skull." In Hebrew it was called "Golgotha." There they crucified him and two others with him. One was on either side, with Jesus between them. (John 19:17-18)*

RELATED VERSES: *Matthew 27:32–28:20; Mark 15:16-47; Luke 23:26-56*

Q: WHY DOES JESUS WANT US TO FOLLOW HIM?

39

A: Jesus told the people to follow him because he is the way to God, heaven, and eternal life. When Jesus was on earth, the disciples and others followed him by walking close to him and listening to his words. Today, we follow Jesus by copying his example and by doing what he says.

KEY VERSES: *Then Jesus said to the disciples, "Do you want to be my followers? If you do, you must deny yourselves. You must take up your cross and follow me. For anyone who keeps his life for himself shall lose it. And anyone who loses his life for me shall find it again. What good is it if you gain the whole world and lose eternal life? What could ever be as good as eternal life?" (Matthew 16:24-26)*

RELATED VERSES: *Matthew 4:19; John 14:6*

Q: WHY DID JESUS GET TEMPTED BY THE DEVIL?

40

A: When someone tempts you, that person is trying to get you to do something. Because Satan is against Jesus, he tried to get Jesus to do something wrong, to sin. But Jesus didn't give in—he didn't sin. Being tempted isn't sin; giving in to temptation is.

KEY VERSES: *This High Priest of ours understands how weak we are. He had the same temptations we do. But he never once gave way to them and sinned. So let us come boldly to the throne of God. There he will give us his mercy. And there we will find grace to help in times of need. (Hebrews 4:15-16)*

RELATED VERSES: *Matthew 4:1-11; Mark 1:12-13; Luke 4:1-13*

RELATED QUESTION: *What does "being tempted" mean?*

Q: WHY DIDN'T GOD JUST FORGIVE EVERYBODY?

41

A: It would not be right or fair for God to just forgive everyone. There is a penalty that must be paid for doing wrong. The penalty for sinning against God is death, eternal death. But God loved us so much that he sent Jesus, his only Son, to pay our penalty. Jesus did this by dying on the cross, in our place. Now everyone can be forgiven by trusting in Christ.

KEY VERSES: *Yes, all have sinned. All fall short of God's perfect glory. But if we trust in Jesus Christ, God says we are "not guilty." In his kindness he freely takes away our sins. God sent Christ Jesus to take the punishment for our sins. He ended all God's anger against us. Christ's blood and our faith saves us from God's anger. This is the way he could be fair to everybody. He did not punish the people who sinned before Christ came. He was looking forward to the time when Christ would come and take away those sins. (Romans 3:23-25)*

RELATED VERSES: *Mark 8:31; John 3:16; Romans 5:8; Hebrews 2:14-17; 8:3; 9:13-14, 22-23; 1 John 1:7*

RELATED QUESTION: *Why did Jesus have to die?*

SALVATION

Q: WHY DO GOD AND JESUS LOVE PEOPLE?

42

A: God loves us because that's what he decided to do. God doesn't love us because we're good or nice people. In fact, no one could ever be good enough to be worthy of God's love. Isn't it amazing that God loves us even though we sometimes ignore him and disobey him?

KEY VERSE: *But God showed his great love for us. He sent Christ to die for us while we were still sinners. (Romans 5:8)*

RELATED VERSES: *John 1:12; 16:7*

NOTE TO PARENTS: *The best way to help children understand God's love is to demonstrate it to them. Hug them, train them, cheer them, guide them, discipline them, talk to them, spend time with them, accept them, forgive them, help them, stand by them, and provide for them—then they'll understand.*

Q: HOW CAN JESUS FIT IN MY HEART?

43

A: When we say "heart," we mean deep down inside us—where we really feel and believe. So when someone says, "Jesus lives in my heart," the person means that he has asked Jesus to be his Savior— to forgive and take care of him—and that Jesus is in charge of his life. When someone asks Jesus to take over, God really does come inside—the Holy Spirit comes and lives inside that person. And the Holy Spirit can be in all of the people who love God at the same time. Jesus wants to be very close to you, too, like a good friend. Through his Holy Spirit, he wants to "live in your heart."

KEY VERSES: *He has kept this secret for centuries and generations past. But now he is pleased to tell it to the brothers and sisters. The riches and glory of his plan are for you Gentiles, too. This is the secret: Christ in your hearts is your only hope of glory. (Colossians 1:26-27)*

RELATED VERSES: *John 16:7-8; Acts 1:8; 1 Thessalonians 4:8*

RELATED QUESTION: *How can other people have Jesus in their hearts if he's in mine?*

NOTE TO PARENTS: *Children are often told that Jesus comes to live inside their hearts when they believe in him. Young children take this literally and think that a miniaturized Jesus actually lives in their chest. "Jesus lives in my heart" is a shorthand way of calling Jesus Savior and Lord. "Jesus goes with you everywhere" may be a better way of phrasing it for young children.*

Q: HOW DO YOU GET JESUS IN YOUR HEART?

44

A: You become a Christian by asking Jesus to take over your life. You know that you have done wrong things, that you have sinned, and you recognize that you need Jesus to forgive your sins. So you tell Jesus about your sins and that you are sorry, and you ask for his forgiveness. Then you do what Jesus says.

KEY VERSES: *But now God has shown us another way to Heaven. It is not by "being good enough" and trying to keep his laws. It is by a new way. It is not really new. Because the Scriptures told about it long ago. Now God says he will accept us and declare us "not guilty." He will do this if we trust Jesus Christ to take away our sins. We all can be saved by coming to Christ. It doesn't matter who we are or what we have been like. Yes, all have sinned. All fall short of God's perfect glory. But if we trust in Jesus Christ, God says we are "not guilty." In his kindness he freely takes away our sins. (Romans 3:21-24)*

RELATED VERSES: *John 5:24; Acts 19:18; 1 John 1:9*

RELATED QUESTION: *How does someone become a Christian?*

Q: WOULD GOD SEND NICE PEOPLE TO HELL IF THEY ARE NOT CHRISTIANS?

45

A:

Compared to each other, some people are nice and some are mean. But compared to God, all people are not very good. All people need to be forgiven for their sins, not just "mean people." To be fair, God has to punish sin. God doesn't *want* to send anyone to hell. That's why he sent Jesus—to pay the penalty for our sins by dying on the cross. But, unfortunately, not all people are willing to admit that they sin and ask for forgiveness. They don't accept the payment of Jesus' death for them. So God lets them experience the results of their choice.

KEY VERSES: *The Bible says, "No one is good without God. Every person in the world has sinned." No one has ever really followed God's paths or even truly wanted to. Everyone has turned away from God. All have gone wrong. No one anywhere has kept on doing what is right. (Romans 3:10-12)*

RELATED VERSES: *Romans 5:16; Jude 1:4*

RELATED QUESTION: *Who will God send to hell?*

Q: IF I SWEAR, WILL I GO TO HELL WHEN I DIE?

46

A: Although it is very important to watch what we say, God doesn't decide who goes to hell because of our speech. Instead, our forgiveness and eternal life are based on the death and resurrection of Jesus Christ. If we trust Jesus to save us, we are forgiven. Of course that doesn't make it all right to swear. We should always try to speak and do what is right.

KEY VERSES: *Because of his kindness, you have been saved through trusting Christ. And even that trust is not your own. It, too, is a gift from God. Salvation is not a reward for the good we have done. So none of us can take any credit for it. (Ephesians 2:8-9)*

RELATED VERSES: *Romans 3:14; James 3:10*

RELATED QUESTION: *What happens to people who use bad words?*

NOTE TO PARENTS: *Many children think they are too bad or evil to be forgiven by God. If you sense that your child feels this way, he or she needs to know that God can forgive any sin. Tell your children that they are not uniquely bad—all people sin.*

Q: WILL ALL OF MY FRIENDS GO TO HEAVEN?

47

A: God loves your friends just as he loves you. Only God knows who will go to heaven and hell; we don't. But there is only one way to heaven—through Jesus. So we can go to heaven only if we have given our life to Christ. If your friends don't follow Jesus, you can help them understand by telling them the Good News about Jesus and how he died for them. Heaven is worth going to even if your friends don't. There will be no good times in hell.

KEY VERSE: *Jesus said, "I am the Way, the Truth, and the Life. No one can get to the Father except through me." (John 14:6)*

RELATED VERSES: *John 5:24; 11:25; Acts 4:12; 1 John 2:23*

RELATED QUESTION: *Does God love my friends?*

NOTE TO PARENTS: *This may be a good opportunity to encourage your child to invite a friend to church or Sunday school.*

Q: WHY ISN'T EVERYONE A CHRISTIAN?

48

A: Not everyone wants to be a Christian, and God doesn't force people to follow Jesus. Some people don't just reject Christ, they also act mean to Christians. That's because they don't understand the love that God has for them. We should try to tell these people about God's love for them.

KEY VERSES: *[Jesus is praying] "And now I am coming to you. I have told them many things while I was with them. They should be filled with my joy. I have given them your commands. And the world hates them. This is because they don't belong in the world, just as I don't. I'm not asking you to take them out of the world. I am asking that you keep them from the evil one. They are not part of this world any more than I am." (John 17:13-16)*

RELATED VERSES: *Matthew 7:14; John 15:9*

RELATED QUESTION: *Why do some people laugh when I talk about Jesus?*

NOTE TO PARENTS: *You can pray with your child for others to become Christians.*

Q: WHY DOESN'T GOD JUST ZAP THE BAD PEOPLE?

49

A: God loves people so much, even the worst people in the world, that he is giving them time to turn away from being bad and to turn to him. God is very patient. Someday, however, the time will be up, and all those who refuse to live God's way and give their lives to Christ will be punished. That will be a very sad day, but it will come.

KEY VERSE: *It may seem like he is slow in coming back as he promised. But he isn't. He is waiting because he does not want anyone to die. He is giving more time for sinners to repent. (2 Peter 3:9)*

RELATED VERSES: *Matthew 13:24-30; Hebrews 10:23*

RELATED QUESTION: *Why do people get away with being bad?*

Q: HOW LONG IS ETERNITY?

50

A: We can't even imagine how long eternity is. Eternity goes on forever. Sometimes we have good times that we wish would never end—such as a party or a vacation or a visit by a friend from out of town. But they do come to an end. Eternity, however, never ends. God is eternal, and he has given us eternal life. If we know Jesus, we will live forever with him, someday in heaven, after our life on earth comes to an end.

KEY VERSE: *But don't forget this, dear friends! A day is like 1,000 years to the Lord. (2 Peter 3:8)*

RELATED VERSES: *Psalm 41:13; 90:4; 1 Timothy 1:17*

RELATED QUESTION: *What is eternity?*

Q: WHAT DOES GOD WANT US TO DO?

51

A: In the Bible, God's Word, God tells us what he
wants us to do, how he wants us to live.
Although there are a lot of messages and information in
the Bible, God's four main instructions for our lives are:
(1) believe in Jesus and trust him every day; (2) obey
Jesus and do what he says; (3) love God and others;
(4) be fair and honest and live for God without being
proud about it.

KEY VERSES: *They replied, "What should we do to satisfy
God?" Jesus told them, "God's will is that you believe
in the one he has sent." (John 6:28-29)*

RELATED VERSES: *Ecclesiastes 12:13-14; Micah 6:6-8;
Matthew 19:19; 22:39*

RELATED QUESTION: *How can I know what God wants me
to do?*

PRAYER

Q: IF GOD GIVES US EVERYTHING WE ASK FOR, THEN HOW COME WE DON'T HAVE EVERYTHING?

52

A: God doesn't give us everything we *ask* for. He gives us everything we *need,* when we need it. Sometimes we want things that could hurt us, such as when a baby wants to play in the fire. God knows what can hurt us, so he doesn't give us those things because he loves us. God wants to give us what is good for us.

KEY VERSE: *When you do ask you don't get it because your whole aim is wrong. You want only what will make you happy. (James 4:3)*

RELATED VERSES: *Matthew 7:7-11; 21:22; Luke 11:9*

RELATED QUESTION: *Why didn't I get what I prayed for?*

NOTE TO PARENTS: *If your child is older, you may want to explain that there are three types of pray-ers: (1) those who don't ask, (2) those who ask with the wrong motives, and (3) those who consider what God wants and pray accordingly. This question may be a chance to find a need that your child has and pray with him or her about it.*

Q: WHY DO WE PRAY?

53

A: Prayer is talking with God. When we have a good friend, we talk to that person about all sorts of things. That's part of being a friend. In the same way, we should talk to God about what is happening in our life. God wants us to share our life with him, to tell him about what makes us happy, sad, and afraid. He wants to know what we want and what we would like him to do, for ourself and for others. Also, when we pray, we open ourself up to God so that he can make good changes in us.

KEY VERSES: *Don't worry about anything. Instead, pray about everything. Tell God your needs, and don't forget to thank him for his answers. If you do this, you will find God's peace. It is far more wonderful than the human mind can understand. God's peace will keep your thoughts and your hearts as you trust in Christ Jesus. (Philippians 4:6-7)*

RELATED VERSES: *Luke 6:12; Acts 6:1-4; Ephesians 6:12-13; James 4:2*

RELATED QUESTION: *What is prayer?*

NOTE TO PARENTS: Practical Christianity *(LaVonne Neff and others, Tyndale House Publishers) and* What Is Prayer? *(Carolyn Nystrom, Moody Press) are two good resources for more on the topic of prayer.*

Q: WILL GOD GIVE CHILDREN TOYS IF THEY ASK HIM FOR THEM?

54

A: Some people think God is there to give us toys and other things we want. But God doesn't just hand out stuff to us. His purpose is to make us into people who are like Christ. God really cares about us, and he knows what we need. Although toys seem important sometimes, there are other things that we need more. God also doesn't want us to get our happiness from toys, but from him and from other people.

KEY VERSES: *You want what you don't have. So you kill to get it! You long for what others have. So you start a fight to take it away! Why don't you have what you want? Because you don't ask God for it. When you do ask you don't get it because your whole aim is wrong. You want only what will make you happy. (James 4:2-3)*

RELATED VERSES: *Philippians 4:4-10; 1 Thessalonians 5:17*

RELATED QUESTIONS: *If I pray for something, will God give it to me? Does God care about me?*

Q: WHAT SHOULD I SAY TO GOD WHEN I PRAY?

55

A: When we pray, it's easy to say the same words over and over. Prayer can become a habit that we don't think about. Instead, we should think about what we are saying when we pray, and we should be honest with God. Also, we shouldn't pray to show off, but we should say to God what we want to tell him. The Lord's Prayer can be a guide for what to talk to God about. Prayers can include thanking God for who he is and for what he has done. In prayer we can confess our sins, telling God that we are sorry for the bad things we have done. We can make requests, too, asking God to help others and to give us strength and guidance. We can talk to God about anything on our mind.

KEY VERSES: *[Jesus is speaking] "Pray like this: 'Our Father in Heaven, we honor your holy name. We ask that your kingdom will come now. May your will be done here on earth, just as it is in Heaven. Give us our food again today, as usual. And forgive us our sins, just as we have forgiven those who have sinned against us. Don't bring us into temptation. But keep us safe from the Evil One. Amen.'" (Matthew 6:9-13)*

RELATED VERSES: *Luke 11:1-13; Philippians 4:6; 1 Thessalonians 5:17; 1 Timothy 2:8; James 5:16*

NOTE TO PARENTS: *Children can get caught into a routine prayer. Look for ways to vary the family prayers in which your children participate. For example, you could suggest that each member of the family pray about what happened during the day, or you could compile a family prayer list and use it to guide your family prayer times.*

Q: HOW COME WHEN I PRAY TO GOD HE DOESN'T ALWAYS ANSWER?

Hello—you've reached heaven's 1-800 number. There isn't anyone here to take your call right now, but if you leave a long message at the sound of the choir, we will return your call. This is a recording...

56

A: There's a difference between hearing and answering. God hears all our prayers, but he doesn't always give us what we ask for. Also, he answers all our prayers, but not always the way we want him to. When we ask God for something, sometimes he answers no or wait. A good answer is not always yes.

KEY VERSES: *Yes, the Lord hears the good man when he calls for help. He saves him out of all his troubles. The Lord is close to those whose hearts are breaking. He saves those who are sorry for their sins. The good man does not escape all troubles. But the Lord helps him in each and every one. (Psalm 34:17-19)*

RELATED VERSES: *Psalm 139:4; 2 Corinthians 12:8; 1 Peter 5:7*

RELATED QUESTION: *Does God always hear my prayers?*

Q: WHY DID I HAVE A BAD DREAM WHEN I PRAYED BEFORE I WENT TO SLEEP?

57

A: It's good to pray before falling asleep at night. Praying helps us think through the day and thank God for how much he loves us. We should also pray for the next day. Christians aren't promised that they will be free from all problems and difficulties. God does promise to be with us during hard times. A lot of things can cause bad dreams—something on our mind, something we ate, a noise. Ask God to help you sleep, but remember that whatever happens, he is there with you.

KEY VERSE: *Then I lay down and slept in peace and woke up safely. For the Lord was watching over me. (Psalm 3:5)*

RELATED VERSES: *Psalm 34:17-19; 139:7-11; Proverbs 3:24-26; Matthew 2:12-13; Acts 2:17*

RELATED QUESTION: *If God is with me, why did he let me have a bad dream?*

Q: HOW CAN GOD HEAR EVERYONE'S PRAYERS AT ONCE?

58

A: God can hear everyone's prayers at once because God is everywhere. We can only be in one place at a time, and usually we can't understand more than one person at a time. But God is not like us—he is not limited. Not only can God hear and understand everyone who is praying to him in many different languages, but he also can give each person his full attention. Isn't that great?

KEY VERSES: *[God is speaking] "Am I a God who is only in one place? Do they think I cannot see what they are doing? Can anyone hide from me? Am I not everywhere in Heaven and earth at the same time?" (Jeremiah 23:23-24)*

RELATED VERSES: *Luke 1:13; Acts 10:31*

RELATED QUESTION: *How can God hear people praying at the same time from different countries?*

NOTE TO PARENTS: *Many children harbor the misconception that God is limited as we are. This is partly unavoidable because children think concretely. But it is also an opportunity for you to introduce them to the idea that God is infinitely greater than we are. He can even hear thousands of prayers at once! An illustration that might help: When five people touch you, you can feel all five.*

HEAVEN

AND

HELL

Q: IF WE WENT HIGH ENOUGH IN THE SKY, WOULD WE FIND HEAVEN?

59

A: No one but God knows exactly where heaven is. But the best way we can describe its location is to say it is "up." If we rode a spaceship up, way out into space, we would not find heaven—it can't be seen or found by people. Only God can take us there. And that's what he does, after we die, if we have trusted in Jesus as our Savior.

KEY VERSES: *Not long after this, Jesus rose into the sky. He went up into a cloud, leaving them staring after him. They were straining their eyes for another look at him. But suddenly two white-robed men were standing there with them. They said, "Men of Galilee, why are you standing here staring at the sky? Jesus has gone to Heaven. And someday he will come back again, just as he went!" (Acts 1:9-11)*

RELATED VERSES: *John 3:13; Luke 24:50-51*

RELATED QUESTIONS: *Where is heaven? Is heaven up?*

Q: **WHAT IS HEAVEN LIKE?**

60

A: The Bible uses some wonderful pictures to tell us what heaven is like. In our world, we think that gold is important because it's so valuable. But in heaven, the streets will be gold—we'll *walk* on it. The best way to picture heaven is to imagine the most exciting and fun place that you've ever been to. Heaven will be like that only much, much better. Jesus told his followers that he was leaving earth to go to heaven to prepare a place for them. He has a special place for us, where there is no crying or sadness and we will be filled with joy.

KEY VERSES: *[Jesus is speaking] "There are many homes in my Father's house. I am going to prepare a place for you. I will come again and take you to me. Then you will be with me where I am about to go. If this weren't so, I would tell you plainly." (John 14:2-3)*

RELATED VERSES: *Isaiah 60:17; Revelation 21:21*

RELATED QUESTIONS: *What will we do in heaven? Are the streets in heaven real gold or just painted gold?*

Q: IS THERE A MCDONALD'S IN HEAVEN?

61

A: No. In heaven, we won't need people to work to make us food. Our bodies will be different. They will be "glorified," or perfect, bodies. We don't know if we will eat there or what kind of food we will need. God will make sure that we have everything we need. Heaven will be fun. It will be great!

KEY VERSES: *[When Jesus appeared to the disciples] Still they stood there, unsure. They were filled with joy and doubt. Then he asked them, "Do you have anything here to eat?" They gave him a piece of broiled fish. And he ate it as they watched! (Luke 24:41-43)*

RELATED VERSES: *Romans 16:18; Philippians 3:19*

RELATED QUESTIONS: *What do we eat in heaven? Are there going to be things I enjoy in heaven? Is there school in heaven?*

NOTE TO PARENTS: *Children are concerned about food. Food is important to them, and they don't want to be hungry. Curiosity about what they will be eating in heaven may underlie questions like these.*

Q: WILL THERE BE TOYS IN HEAVEN?

R.I.P.
BORN
Dec. 25
DIED
Jan. 3

62

A: We like toys because we have such fun with them. But we can get tired of toys, too. For example, you don't play with your baby toys any more. That's because you outgrew them and got tired of them. God will have just the right kind of toys for you in heaven. You will enjoy heaven even more than your favorite toys.

KEY VERSES: *When I was a child I thought like a child does. When I became a man I put away the childish things. We can see and understand only a little about God now. It is like we were looking at his reflection in a poor mirror. Someday we are going to see him face to face. Now all that I know is hazy and blurred. But then I will see everything clearly. I will see as clearly as God sees into my heart right now. (1 Corinthians 13:11-12)*

RELATED VERSES: *Ephesians 4:14; 1 Corinthians 14:20*

RELATED QUESTIONS: *Will I have my teddy bear in heaven? Do toys go to heaven?*

Q: WILL MY PET GO TO HEAVEN WHEN IT DIES?

63

A: We don't know what happens to animals when they die, but God does, and we know his plan is good. Sometimes we may get the idea that animals think and understand as we do. But God created animals different from people. Animals don't have souls or think as we do, so they can't enjoy God the way we can. Here on earth, pets are fun to play with and animals are interesting to watch. Only God knows if pets will join us in heaven.

KEY VERSES: *God made all sorts of wild animals and cattle and reptiles. And God was pleased with what he had done. Then God said, "Let us make a man—someone like ourselves. He will be the master of all life upon the earth and in the skies and in the seas." So God made man like his Maker. Like God did God make man. Man and maid did he make them. (Genesis 1:25-27)*

RELATED VERSES: *Isaiah 11:6-8; 65:25*

RELATED QUESTION: *Where do animals go when they die?*

NOTE TO PARENTS: *This question may be a way of testing the reality of heaven. A child's world is tied to his or her pet, and the death of a pet naturally raises the question of what happens to it afterward. But if you're not sure how to answer, don't be afraid of saying you don't know. The answer may not be as important as helping your child deal with losing a pet. When we get to heaven, God will give us everything we need to be filled with unspeakable joy.*

Q: WHY CAN'T WE GO TO HEAVEN AND JUST SEE IT AND THEN COME BACK?

64

A: This question is like asking, "Can I become a teenager and then come back to my age right now?" It's impossible because you have to *grow* into your teens; you can't simply jump there and back. In the same way, heaven is more than a place you can visit. It's a time at the end of life, and God has to make us ready to go there. In fact, we have to change in order to go there. We know that heaven exists because God has told us so in his Word, the Bible. And Jesus promised to "prepare a place" so that we can live with him forever (John 14:2). Once we get there, we won't want to come back.

KEY VERSES: *Then I looked and saw a door standing open in Heaven. I heard the same voice I had heard before. It was the one that sounded like a mighty trumpet blast. It said, "Come up! I will show you what must happen in the future!" And instantly I was in the spirit. And I saw a throne and someone sitting on it! Great bursts of light flashed forth from him. It was like light from a glittering diamond or from a shining ruby. There was a rainbow glowing like an emerald around his throne. (Revelation 4:1-3)*

RELATED VERSES: *Exodus 33:22; Matthew 17:2; 2 Corinthians 12:2-3*

RELATED QUESTIONS: *Is heaven really there? Why can't I go to heaven now? How do we get to heaven after we die?*

Q: WILL I HAVE MY SAME NAME IN HEAVEN?

65

A: When we get to heaven, we will see our friends and family members who have died and gone there before us. They will recognize us, and we will know them. The Bible says that when we trust Christ as Savior, our names are written in the "Book of Life." That's God's list of who gets into heaven.

KEY VERSE: *[Jesus is speaking] "All who conquer will be dressed in white. I will not erase their names from the Book of Life. I will announce before my Father and his angels that they are mine." (Revelation 3:5)*

RELATED VERSES: *Isaiah 62:1-3; Luke 16:19-24*

RELATED QUESTIONS: *Will people know me in heaven? Will I remember my family and friends in heaven? Will life in heaven be like it is here? Will I stay the same in heaven as I am here?*

Q: WILL GOD LET ME VISIT GRANDPA IN HEAVEN?

66

A: One of the great things about going to heaven is getting to see the people we love and want to see. If those people have trusted in Christ, they will be there. If your grandpa is in heaven, you will be able to see him when you go there.

KEY VERSES: *The believers who are dead will be the first to rise to meet the Lord. Then we who are alive and remain on the earth will be caught up with them. We will go to the clouds to meet the Lord in the air. We will stay with him forever. So comfort and cheer each other with this news. (1 Thessalonians 4:16-18)*

RELATED VERSES: *Daniel 7:13; Matthew 17:1-3; Acts 7:56*

RELATED QUESTION: *Why did God take Grandpa to heaven?*

NOTE TO PARENTS: *If a grandparent has died recently, your child will have many questions like this one. He or she may also want to express grief over the loss. Be open to talk to your child about his or her feelings.*

Q: WHY IS HELL DARK IF THEY HAVE FIRES?

67

A: The Bible uses a lot of pictures to give us an idea of what heaven and hell are like. Fire means burning and pain. Do you remember having a fever? You felt like you were burning up, but there was no flame. Darkness means loneliness. Can you imagine anything more lonely than sitting by yourself in total darkness? What God is telling us is that hell is a terrible place. We certainly don't want to go there.

KEY VERSE: *[Jesus is speaking] "And many . . . shall be thrown into outer darkness. They will be put in the place of crying and pain." (Matthew 8:12)*

RELATED VERSES: *Luke 16:28; Revelation 20:15*

RELATED QUESTIONS: *What's really happening in hell? What is hell like?*

NOTE TO PARENTS: *Children hear conflicting descriptions of hell. They hear that hell is a dark place (Matthew 8:12) and yet a lake of fire (Revelation 19:20). (They may also have heard that it is cold.) Instead of grasping the meanings of these metaphors, the child is taking the images concretely.*

Q: WHO ENDS UP IN HELL?

68

A: Hell is the place where God will punish Satan and his followers—and all those who refuse to follow God. We don't know exactly who will go there because we don't make that judgment, God does. But God has made it possible for everyone to escape punishment in hell. He gives everyone the opportunity to go to heaven. That's why he sent Jesus to die on the cross. When Jesus suffered and died, he took our place—he paid the penalty for our sins. So if we trust in Jesus, we can escape hell and go to heaven. It sure would be great if all our friends, family, and neighbors would end up in heaven. Let's tell them how to get there.

KEY VERSE: *Anyone whose name wasn't in the Book of Life was thrown into the Lake of Fire. (Revelation 20:15)*

RELATED VERSES: *John 3:16-18; 1 John 1:9*

RELATED QUESTIONS: *Are there kids in hell? Who goes to hell? Will I go to hell if I swear?*

ANGELS
AND
DEMONS

Q: WHAT DO ANGELS REALLY LOOK LIKE?

69

A: The word *angel* means "messenger." Angels are God's messengers. They can also be God's warriors. In the Bible we read about people who saw angels. Sometimes the people knew they were angels, and sometimes they didn't. Some angels described in the Bible have wings. Those angels are called cherubim. But most of the angels in the Bible stories looked like regular people. We don't know what angels look like in heaven.

KEY VERSES: *I, John, saw and heard all these things. I fell down to worship the angel who showed them to me. But he said, "No, don't do anything like that. I am a servant of Jesus like you, and like your brothers the prophets. I am like all those who hear and act on the truth stated in this book. Only worship God." (Revelation 22:8-9)*

RELATED VERSES: *Genesis 19:1; Hebrews 13:2*

RELATED QUESTIONS: *Are angels boys or girls? Do angels eat?*

NOTE TO PARENTS: *You may want to ask if your child has seen a picture of an angel, perhaps in a children's Bible, in a painting, in the cartoons, etc. Those pictures often leave mental impressions about an angel's appearance.*

Q: WHEN I DIE, WILL I BECOME AN ANGEL?

70

A: Angels are spiritual beings created by God. They are different from human beings. You are a spiritual being, too. In other words, you have a soul and will live forever and can know God. But you are also a physical being. You live on earth and have a physical body. When you die, you will leave your physical body behind and will be given a glorified or perfect body in heaven. We don't know exactly what our glorified bodies will be like, but we know that people in heaven will be able to recognize us. One thing is for sure, we don't become angels when we die. In fact, angels will serve us in heaven. Wow!

KEY VERSE: *Don't you know that we will judge the angels in Heaven? You should be able to decide your problems here on earth easily enough. (1 Corinthians 6:3)*

RELATED VERSES: *Psalm 8:5; Hebrews 2:7*

RELATED QUESTIONS: *How many angels are there? Do you have to die to be a spirit?*

NOTE TO PARENTS: *According to Matthew 26:53 and other passages, there are thousands of angels.*

Q: WHAT DOES MY ANGEL DO?

ROLLER COASTER MADNESS

71

A: Angels are God's helpers. They live in heaven with him. God often instructs angels to protect people by blocking the evil that Satan directs at them. Angels also carry out God's purposes in people's lives. In other words, angels help us do what God wants us to do.

KEY VERSE: *[Jesus is speaking] "Be careful that you don't look down upon a single one of these children. For I tell you that in Heaven their angels can speak directly to my Father." (Matthew 18:10)*

RELATED VERSES: *Genesis 24:7; Numbers 22:15-35; Daniel 3:28; 6:22; Matthew 1:21-24; 4:11; Hebrews 1:14*

RELATED QUESTION: *Are there angels in the room with us?*

NOTE TO PARENTS: *Some people think that each person has a guardian angel, an angel assigned to a person to watch over and protect him or her. We don't know for sure if people have guardian angels. But we do know that God uses angels to accomplish his will.*

Q: WHO IS THE DEVIL?

72

A: The devil is also called Satan. The word *devil* means "liar" or "enemy." Satan used to be an angel. But he wanted to be like God, so he fought against God. God kicked him out of heaven. Ever since then, Satan has worked on earth, trying to defeat God and God's people. He is God's enemy. But God is far stronger than Satan. In the end, Satan will be thrown into hell and suffer forever.

KEY VERSE: *But if you keep on sinning, it shows you belong to Satan. He has been sinning from the beginning. But the Son of God came to destroy the works of the devil. (1 John 3:8)*

RELATED VERSES: *Genesis 3:1-15; 1 Chronicles 21:1; Job 1:6-13; 2:1-7; Zechariah 3:1-2; Matthew 4:1-11; John 14:30; 2 Corinthians 11:14; Ephesians 6:11; Hebrews 2:14*

RELATED QUESTIONS: *Why did God make the devil? Why doesn't God kill Satan? Will God forgive Satan?*

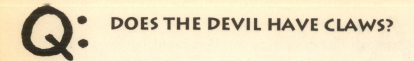

Q: DOES THE DEVIL HAVE CLAWS?

73

A: The devil can take many forms. When he tempted Adam and Eve, he was a serpent. But remember, Satan is an angel and once was an angel of light. So he probably doesn't look like the funny costumes we see at Halloween (all red, with horns and a pitchfork). Instead, the devil usually tries to look like something good and beautiful. Remember, Satan is the father of lies, so he is usually trying to trick us. He'll say that we don't deserve to be God's children and that we are not forgiven. But always remember that God is much stronger than Satan (it's not even a close contest), and God can keep us safe from Satan.

KEY VERSE: *Yet I am not surprised! Satan can change himself into an angel of light. (2 Corinthians 11:14)*

RELATED VERSES: *Job 1:6-13; 2:1-7; Luke 11:4; John 8:44; James 4:7*

RELATED QUESTIONS: *Can the devil hurt me? Is the devil more powerful than God?*

NOTE TO PARENTS: *When children hear about Satan, they may wonder if he can hurt them physically. Of course that's possible, but Satan's attacks are usually much more subtle and focused on keeping people far from God. Usually he tries to get us to center our life around anything but God and to ignore God's commands. Explain to your child that God beats the devil every time and that we can beat Satan too (resist his temptations) if we stay close to God. This means doing what God says, relying on him, and talking to him about everything in our life.*

Q: WHY IS THE DEVIL AFTER US?

74

A: Satan is God's enemy, so he is against anyone who is on God's side. Satan is jealous of our friendship with God—he can't stand it when we spend time with the Lord. And he wants to stop us from obeying God and from doing good. The devil hates God, so he hates us because we love God.

KEY VERSE: *So give yourselves humbly to God. Resist the devil and he will run from you. (James 4:7)*

RELATED VERSES: *Ephesians 6:11; 1 Peter 5:8-9; Revelation 12:9*

Q: WHAT ARE DEMONS?

75

A: Like the devil, demons are bad angels. They followed Satan when he turned against God. Demons are spiritual beings who work and fight against God. Demons are Satan's helpers. There is only one devil, but there are thousands of demons. They are all over the world, trying to keep people from following Christ and obeying God. But God is more powerful than all the demons and the devil put together. God will keep us safe from demons as we trust in him. At the end of time, all demons will be thrown into the Lake of Fire with the devil.

KEY VERSE: *[Jesus is speaking] "Then I will turn to those on my left. I will say, 'Away with you, you cursed ones. Go into the fire prepared for the devil and his demons.'" (Matthew 25:41)*

RELATED VERSES: *Mark 5:9-13; Luke 4:41; 11:15; Revelation 18:2*

NOTE TO PARENTS: *The related verses show that demons are active in the world.*

Q: WILL I EVER GET A DEMON?

76

A: It's easy to get the idea from watching television and hearing kids talk that demons can take over people's lives whenever they want. But that's not true. It is true that some people have demons in them. But demons can only enter people who let them and who are not close to God. And never forget, God is much more powerful than Satan or any of the demons. He can protect us.

KEY VERSES: *When the 70 disciples came back, they gave [Jesus] a joyful report. They said, "Even the demons obey us when we use your name." "Yes," he told them. "I saw Satan falling from Heaven like a flash of light! I have given you the power to walk among snakes and scorpions. And I have given you authority over the power of the Enemy. Nothing shall hurt you! But don't be full of joy because the demons obey you. Be full of joy because your names are written in Heaven." (Luke 10:17-20)*

RELATED VERSES: *Matthew 10:7-8; Romans 8:38-39*

SUFFERING
AND
EVIL

Q: WHY DO SOME PEOPLE DIE BEFORE THEY ARE OLD?

77

A: Death entered the world when sin came in. Ever since Adam and Eve, pain and death have been part of life. Eventually, everything that is alive in our world has to die. Plants die. Animals die. People die. Death can come from a lot of different causes: automobile accidents, sickness, old age, and so forth. And life is short, no matter how long a person lives. Just ask someone who is sixty or seventy or eighty. Remember that because life is short, we should make the most of every day we are alive. Each breath is a gift from God. But also remember that this life is not all there is. After we die we can live forever with God.

KEY VERSES: *For to me, living is Christ, and dying—well, that's better yet! But if I live I can win people to Christ. So I don't know which is better. Should I live or die? Sometimes I want to live, and at other times I don't. For I long to go and be with Christ. How much happier for me than being here! (Philippians 1:21-23)*

RELATED VERSE: *2 Corinthians 5:6*

Q: WHY ARE SOME PEOPLE DIFFERENT FROM OTHERS?

78

A: Bad things happen in this world, and people suffer. Some people are hurt in accidents. Some are injured in sports. Some are born with physical problems. You can probably think of many ways that people can be harmed. Today there are many doctors, nurses, and other people who can help us when we are hurt or need special help. They can give us medicine and bandages, and they can operate if necessary. And scientists are always working on special tools to help. Glasses, wheel chairs, hearing aids, and artificial legs are just a few of their wonderful inventions. These doctors and scientists are gifts from God.

KEY VERSES: *"Master," [Jesus'] disciples asked him, "why was this man born blind? Was it because of his own sins or those of his parents?" "Neither," Jesus answered. "He was born blind to show the power of God." (John 9:2-3)*

RELATED VERSES: *Matthew 5:4; 2 Corinthians 11:30; 12:8-10; 3 John 1:2*

RELATED QUESTION: *Why does God let people have disabilities?*

NOTE TO PARENTS: *God planned for people to be healthy. Disease, death, and disasters are a result of sin in the world. Everyone living in this sinful world suffers the effects of sin, even Christians. God may allow us to go through difficult times to teach us to rely on him or other lessons. Whatever our struggles, God can be glorified in them. In fact, God delights in demonstrating his strength in weak people.*

Q: HOW COME GOD MAKES STORMS WITH LIGHTENING AND THUNDER?

79

A: God made laws that control how the weather works. Thunder storms are part of our weather. Without rain, the grass, flowers, and crops wouldn't grow. The lightening and thunder in those storms come from the electricity in the air and on the earth. Of course, God can interrupt his laws of nature. But he made those laws so the earth would work. God doesn't send storms to scare us or hurt us. But storms can be dangerous, so we should stay out of their way and find cover when they come.

KEY VERSES: *The clouds poured down their rain. The thunder rolled and crackled in the sky. Your lightning flashed. There was thunder in the whirlwind. The lightning lighted up the world! The earth trembled and shook. (Psalm 77:17-18)*

RELATED VERSES: *1 Kings 18:5-45; Psalm 83:15*

RELATED QUESTIONS: *How come God makes weather hurt people or damage stuff? Does God make the weather every day?*

NOTE TO PARENTS: *As mentioned in the note for question 78, many natural disasters are the result of sin in the world. Of course we don't know all the reasons for hurricanes, earthquakes, tornadoes, and other terrible calamities. But some natural disasters are clearly the result of misusing the environment (for example, strip mining) or poor planning (for example, building on a flood plain).*

Q: WHY DOES GOD LET WARS HAPPEN?

80

A: Wars are a result of sin in the world. Because people aren't perfect, sometimes they get angry and fight. When leaders of countries do this, wars start. Wars are like fights between people, only much, much bigger. If people followed God's instructions for living, there would not be wars. God wants people to get along, not to fight and kill each other. But if we ignore God and break his rules, we suffer. God could stop all wars and fights in the world. But God wants human beings to trust him, to listen to him, to obey him, and to live in peace with each other.

KEY VERSES: *What is causing the fights among you? Isn't it because there is a whole army of evil desires within you? You want what you don't have. So you kill to get it! You long for what others have. So you start a fight to take it away! Why don't you have what you want? Because you don't ask God for it. (James 4:1-2)*

RELATED VERSES: *Matthew 24:6; 1 Corinthians 13:4-8*

RELATED QUESTION: *Does God make bad things happen?*

Q: WHY DOES GOD LET US GET SICK?

81

A: Sometimes sickness is the body's way of telling us that we should stop living a certain way. Perhaps we ate too much (or we ate something bad), or we didn't get enough sleep. Sickness and disease are problems that came into the world with sin. All kinds of people get sick: good and bad, rich and poor, old and young. God wants us to take care of ourself and be healthy so we can live for him. And when we are sick, we can pray to God and ask him to help us.

KEY VERSES: *Is anyone sick? He should call for the elders of the church. They should pray over him and pour a little oil upon him. They should call on the Lord to heal him. If their prayer is offered in faith, it will heal him. The Lord will make him well. If his sickness was caused by some sin, the Lord will forgive him. (James 5:14-15)*

RELATED VERSES: *Romans 5:3; 8:28; 2 Corinthians 12:8-9*

Q: IF WE ARE RUNNING OUT OF TREES, WHY DOESN'T GOD JUST MAKE MORE?

82

A: God *is* making more trees, but it is up to us not to use them faster than he replaces them. Some trees are cut down and used for wood, paper, and other products. Other trees are cut down to make room for houses, shopping centers, roads, and other construction projects. Some people say that we are running out of trees. When God created trees and other plants, he made them with the ability to make new ones. They do this by producing seeds that fall to the ground or are planted and then grow. But it takes many years for a tree to grow to be big and tall. So people should be careful not to cut down more trees than can be replaced by the seeds. God has given human beings the job of taking care of the earth. This includes using the trees wisely and planting new ones.

KEY VERSE: *Then God said, "Let us make a man—someone like ourselves. He will be the master of all life upon the earth and in the skies and in the seas." (Genesis 1:26)*

RELATED VERSES: *Deuteronomy 20:19; Revelation 7:3*

NOTE TO PARENTS: *Faithful stewards of the earth are sensitive to the environment. This kind of question is an opportunity for you to teach your children to take good care of God's earth and its resources.*

Q: DOES GOD KNOW ABOUT PEOPLE WHO ARE HUNGRY?

83

A: God knows everything. He even knows how many hairs you have on your head. God knows about all the hungry people in the world, and it makes him sad. Remember, he put *us* in charge of the world. God wants us to care about people and help those who need it. This includes helping to feed those who are hungry. Think about what you can do to feed the hungry people in your community.

KEY VERSES: *He is the God who made both earth and heaven. He made the seas and all that is in them. He is the God who keeps every promise. He gives justice to the poor. He gives food to the hungry. He sets the prisoners free. (Psalm 146:6-7)*

RELATED VERSES: *Matthew 10:29-31; Acts 27:34*

RELATED QUESTION: *Why doesn't God make enough food for everyone?*

Q: WHY DO BROTHERS AND SISTERS FIGHT?

84

A: Part of what it means to be a human being is to be sinful. In other words, no one in this world is perfect. We all do wrong things—we act in ways that displease God and that get us into trouble. Sinfulness causes us to get on each other's nerves and to get angry with one another. We even argue and fight with people we love, like our parents or our brothers and sisters. God has given us rules for living. If we follow his rules, we will get along with each other.

KEY VERSES: *At harvest time Cain brought the Lord a gift of his farm produce. Abel brought the fatty cuts of meat from his best lambs, and presented them to the Lord. The Lord accepted Abel's offering, but not Cain's. This made Cain dejected and very angry. His face grew dark with fury. "Why are you angry?" the Lord asked him. "Why is your face so dark with rage? It can be bright with joy if you will do what you should! But if you refuse to obey, watch out. Sin is waiting to attack you. It is longing to destroy you. But you can conquer it!" (Genesis 4:3-7)*

RELATED VERSES: *Genesis 4:8; James 4:1*

RELATED QUESTIONS: *Why are some people so mean? Why did God give me mean brothers and sisters?*

Q: WHY DO YOU GET MAD AT ME IF YOU HAVE JESUS IN YOUR HEART?

85

A: Not all anger is wrong. We should be angry with the bad things in the world, and we should try to make them right. When children disobey their parents and do other things that are wrong, sometimes their parents get angry. Good parents want their children to do what is right, and so they try to teach children right from wrong. Sometimes, of course, parents get angry at children for the wrong reasons. Maybe the parents are grouchy because they've had a bad day. Or maybe they misunderstood what their child did. Parents are human too; they can make mistakes. Even Christian parents who have God living in them and guiding them can do what is wrong at times. That happens when they don't do what God wants them to do. No matter how your parents act, you should love them and pray for them.

KEY VERSE: *If you are angry, don't sin by staying angry. Don't let the sun go down with you still angry. Get over it quickly. (Ephesians 4:26)*

RELATED VERSES: *Ecclesiastes 3:7-8; Romans 7:14; Colossians 3:5-8*

Q: WHAT IS EVIL?

86

A: Evil is another word for what is bad or sinful. Evil is anything that goes against God and displeases him. This includes a selfish attitude, bad actions, and ignoring God. Evil entered the world when Adam and Eve sinned in the Garden of Eden. You can read that story in the book of Genesis in the Bible. Ever since then, humans have been born wanting to do what is wrong. That's called our "sinful nature." So evil in the world comes from sinful human beings doing what comes naturally. Evil also comes directly from Satan. He is the enemy of God. The devil tries to get people to turn against God and disobey him. The good news is that we can overcome evil in ourself and in the world by giving our life to Jesus. God is far greater than Satan.

KEY VERSE: *Keep away from every kind of evil.*
(1 Thessalonians 5:22)

RELATED VERSES: *Genesis 2:9; Matthew 12:34-35*

RELATED QUESTIONS: *What is sin? How do we displease God?*

THE
CHURCH

Q: WHY DO WE GO TO CHURCH IF GOD IS EVERYWHERE?

87

A: In the Bible, God tells us to join other Christians and worship him. We should spend time alone, praying and reading his Word. But it is also very important to get together with others who follow Christ. We can encourage and strengthen each other. We can pray for each other. We can learn from each other. We can sing and praise God together. We can serve and help each other. All of this can happen in church. Church is also a place where Christians of all ages and types can come together—babies, grandparents, children, poor, wealthy, brown, black, white, American, Asian, African, weak, strong, and so on. Something very special happens when God's family gets together.

KEY VERSE: *Let us not neglect our church meetings, as some people do. Encourage and warn each other. Do this especially now that his day of coming is near. (Hebrews 10:25)*

RELATED VERSES: *1 Chronicles 16:29; Acts 2:42-47; 1 Corinthians 11:23-25; 12:12-31*

RELATED QUESTION: *Why do we have to go to church?*

NOTE TO PARENTS: *Many children find church boring. That's because the service is usually geared for adults. But it also may be because children have not been taught how to worship. Take time to explain the purpose behind the church programs (like Sunday school, church dinners, the worship service, and so forth) and each part of the worship service (for example, songs, Communion, offering, and so forth). Help your child understand what he or she should be doing and why.*

Q: WHY DO WE WORSHIP GOD?

88

A: Worship means praising and thanking God for who he is and for what he has done. People worship in many different ways. Worship can involve group singing, group reading, special music, giving money, prayer, Communion, Bible reading, teaching, preaching, and other activities. God has given us everything good that we have. He loves us and wants the very best for us. Shouldn't we spend time with him and tell him how grateful we are? We play with our friends because we enjoy them. We worship God because we enjoy him.

KEY VERSES: *Jesus replied, "Something new is coming. Then we will not worry about whether to worship here or in Jerusalem. For it's not where we worship that counts, but how we worship. We must worship in spirit and in truth. For God is Spirit, and we must worship him in truth." (John 4:21-24)*

RELATED VERSES: *Exodus 20:3; 1 Chronicles 16:29*

RELATED QUESTION: *Why do we have to do something that isn't fun?*

Q: HOW COME MY FRIENDS GO TO A DIFFERENT CHURCH?

89

A: In most homes, parents decide where children will go to church if they go. Some people go to a certain church because they grew up in that church. Even after moving across town, they drive there every Sunday to be with friends and family. Some people choose a church because they enjoy a certain style of worship. There are many reasons for choosing a church. But some churches really aren't true churches according to the Bible's teachings. Real churches honor Jesus, study God's Word, tell people to give their lives to Christ, and emphasize obeying God. Churches are groups of God's people, meeting together to worship, fellowship, serve, and learn.

KEY VERSES: *If someone says, "I love God," but hates his brother, he is a liar. He doesn't love his brother who is right there in front of him. So how can he love God whom he has never seen? And God said that one must love not only God but his brother too. (1 John 4:20-21)*

RELATED VERSES: *Acts 2:1; Hebrews 10:24-25*

RELATED QUESTION: *Why are there different types of churches?*

Q: WHAT PART OF THE BODY OF CHRIST AM I?

90

A: The Bible uses word pictures to explain how Christians relate to each other. We are a "family," with brothers and sisters in Christ. We are a "building," with Christ as the cornerstone. We are a "body," with each person serving as a special part. God talks about us being a body to show how Christians should treat each other and work together. God has given each Christian special gifts. That means each of us has talents and abilities that can be used to help other believers. Not everybody has the same gifts. And, like the parts of a body, we need each other. All of our gifts are important.

KEY VERSES: *There are many parts to our bodies. It is the same with Christ's body. We are all parts of his body. It takes every one of us to make it complete. We each have different work to do. We belong to each other, and each needs all the others. (Romans 12:4-5)*

RELATED VERSES: *Romans 12:6-8; 1 Corinthians 12:1-30*

NOTE TO PARENTS: *This is a question usually asked only by older children (junior high or older) who have heard teaching on the body of Christ. Encourage them to get involved with a gift or talent they have.*

Q: WHY DO PEOPLE GET BAPTIZED?

BAPTISMAL
TANK

91

A: People get baptized because Jesus was baptized, and they want to follow his example. They also get baptized because Jesus told his followers to go into all the world, telling people about him and baptizing them. Some Christians believe that babies from Christian families should be baptized to show that they belong to Christ. Some Christians think that only believers in Christ should be baptized, to show that Jesus is their Savior. Either way, baptism is a very important event in a Christian's life.

KEY VERSE: *And Peter replied, "Each one of you must turn from sin and come back to God. Then you must be baptized in the name of Jesus Christ. For through him, you will find forgiveness for your sins. Then you also shall be given this gift, the Holy Spirit." (Acts 2:38)*

RELATED VERSES: *Matthew 3:13-17; 28:19*

Q: WHAT HAPPENS TO PEOPLE WHO DON'T GO TO CHURCH?

92

A: Going to church doesn't get a person into heaven. And not going to church doesn't send a person to hell. A person becomes a Christian by faith—believing in Christ—not by doing good things. Most Christians go to church because of what happens there. At church you can meet other Christians. You can find help for your problems and encouragement. You can learn from God's Word and help others. And you can experience wonderful worship, singing, and praying that glorifies God. People who don't go to church miss all that. They miss a very special meeting with God.

KEY VERSES: *Then what can we brag about doing to earn our salvation? Nothing at all! Why? Because we were not forgiven because of our good deeds. Instead, we were forgiven because of what Christ has done and our faith in him. So we are saved by faith in Christ, not by the good things we do. (Romans 3:27-28)*

RELATED VERSES: *Ephesians 2:8-9; Hebrews 10:24-25*

RELATED QUESTION: *Does God send people to hell if they don't go to church?*

Q: WHEN IS JESUS COMING BACK?

93

A: Before Jesus left the earth many years ago, he promised to return some day. And after Jesus went up into the clouds, angels said he would come back eventually. No one knows exactly when that will happen. It could be any day now. For Christians, this is a wonderful event to look forward to. Christ's return will be the beginning of the end for Satan and all evil in the world. Won't it be great to see Jesus in person! Although no one knows when Christ will return, he told us to be ready. This means living the way he would want us to, using our time wisely, and telling others about God's Good News.

KEY VERSES: *[Jesus is speaking] "But no one knows the date and hour when the end will be. Not even the angels know this. No, not even God's Son knows this. Only the Father knows. . . . So be ready at all times. For you don't know what day your Lord is coming." (Matthew 24:36, 42)*

RELATED VERSES: *Matthew 24:27, 42-51; John 14:3; 1 Corinthians 1:7; Colossians 3:4; 1 Thessalonians 5:2-3; 2 Thessalonians 2:1-3; 2 Peter 3:12-13; Revelation 22:20*

RELATED QUESTION: *When can we really see Jesus?*

THE
BIBLE

Q: HOW DID THEY WRITE THE OLD TESTAMENT IF THERE WEREN'T ANY PAPER OR PENCILS?

94

A: When the oldest books in the Bible were written, they didn't have typewriters, computers, or printing presses. And there weren't any ballpoint pens, felt-tipped pens, or number-two pencils. But the people who lived back then did have other tools for writing. The paper they used was different, too. The paper they first wrote the Old Testament on was probably either *papyrus* or *parchment*. Papyrus paper was made from a plant that grows in Bible lands. Parchment was made of animal skin. Either of these could be sewn into long pieces and rolled up into scrolls. Museums have some of these ancient scrolls. You may want to visit a museum and see one.

KEY VERSES: *After the king burned the scroll, the Lord spoke to Jeremiah. He said, "Get another scroll. Write everything again just as you did before." (Jeremiah 36:27-28)*

RELATED VERSES: *Exodus 24:12; 2 Timothy 4:13; 2 Peter 1:20-21*

Q: WHO WROTE THE BIBLE?

95

A: The words in the Bible came from God. That's why it is called "God's Word." God used people to write down the ideas, thoughts, teachings, and words that he wanted to put in the Bible. The writers were very special people, chosen by God for this very important task. And God used many people, writing over many, many years. These people wrote in their own style and in their own language, but they wrote God's Word. God guided their thoughts as they wrote. And God made sure that what they wrote was exactly what he wanted. He kept them from making any mistakes. Today we can read the Bible, God's Word, which he wrote through those special people so many years ago.

KEY VERSES: *No prophecy in the Bible was thought up by the prophet himself. The Holy Spirit within these godly men gave them true messages from God. (2 Peter 1:20-21)*

RELATED VERSES: *Exodus 31:18; 2 Timothy 4:13*

RELATED QUESTIONS: *How was the Bible made? Why did God ask certain people to write the Bible?*

Q: HOW DO WE KNOW THAT WHAT THE BIBLE SAYS IS TRUE?

96

A: The Bible is true because it is God's Word, and God always speaks the truth. When you read the Bible, you will see that it says it is the Word of God. The Bible also says that every word in it is true. But if that doesn't convince you, read the Bible and see for yourself that everything makes sense. When you read it, you will think, *This sounds right! This is true.* The Bible has also proven to be true over the many hundreds of years since it was written. For example, many events predicted in the Bible have happened, just as it said they would.

KEY VERSE: *The whole Bible was given to us by inspiration from God. It is useful to teach us what is true. It helps us to know what is wrong in our lives. It straightens us out and helps us do what is right. (2 Timothy 3:16)*

RELATED VERSES: *John 10:34-36; Hebrews 4:12; 2 Peter 3:15-16*

RELATED QUESTION: *Did the Bible stories really happen or are they like fairy tales?*

NOTE TO PARENTS: *Children usually will not raise this question as a matter of curiosity until they are older. Most will only ask a question like this if they are (1) mocked for believing the Bible, or (2) don't want to do something God wants them to do. If your children ask it, you might want to probe further before or after answering.*

Q: WHY DO WE HAVE THE BIBLE?

97

A: God gave us the Bible because he wanted to talk to us in a way that we would understand. Because God gave us his Word in a book, we can read it over and over. We can share it with a friend. The Bible is like a map—it shows us the direction to go in life. The Bible is like a love letter—it tells us about God's love for us. The Bible is like food—it gives us strength to live. To find out what God is like and how he wants us to live, read the Bible.

KEY VERSE: *For whatever God says to us is full of living power. It is sharper than the sharpest sword. It cuts swift and deep into our innermost thoughts and desires. It shows us for what we really are. (Hebrews 4:12)*

RELATED VERSES: *John 5:39-40; 16:13-15; 17:20; 20:30-31; Acts 17:11; 2 Timothy 3:16-17*

Q: WHY DO SOME BIBLES HAVE PICTURES AND SOME DON'T?

98

A: The people who wrote the Bible didn't put pictures in them. But in recent years, the people who print Bibles wanted to help us better understand the Bible stories. So they put pictures at various places in the Bible to help us see what Bible people and places may have looked like. The pictures are drawings or paintings, not photographs. These pictures were made recently—they're not very old. The artists knew what to draw by learning about that part of the world and by reading what the Bible says about how people lived in Bible times.

KEY VERSE: *When you come, bring the coat I left at Troas with Carpus. Also bring the books, but especially bring the parchments. (2 Timothy 4:13)*

RELATED VERSES: *2 Timothy 3:16-17*

RELATED QUESTION: *Why are there different Bibles?*

NOTE TO PARENTS: *In the key verse, Paul was in prison, just before his death when he wrote this letter to Timothy. The "parchments" were copies of the Old Testament Scriptures. With this question, children may also be asking why there are different versions of the Bible or why there is a difference between their Bible storybook and your Bible.*

Q: WHEN DID "BIBLE TIMES" STOP?

99

A:

The last book in the Bible was written about seventy years after the time Jesus lived on earth. That's a very long time ago, almost two thousand years. In one way that's when Bible times stopped. But in other ways we are still in Bible times. God still speaks to us through his Word, he still cares about us, and he still does miracles. We may not see God divide a sea like he did for Moses, and we may not see anyone walk on water like Jesus did, but God still answers prayer and changes lives.

KEY VERSE: *Tell each other when you do wrong. Pray for each other. Then you will be healed. The earnest prayer of a righteous man has great power and wonderful results. (James 5:16)*

RELATED VERSES: *John 20:30-31; Hebrews 1:1-3; 4:7*

RELATED QUESTIONS: *How long ago was the Bible written? When was the Bible made?*

Q: WHY DID BIBLE PEOPLE GIVE THEIR KIDS SUCH FUNNY NAMES?

100

A: In ancient times, especially among the Jewish people, a person's name was very special. Usually it said something about the person or about the parents' dreams for their child. For example, Jedidiah means "lover of God." Sometimes God told prophets to give their children names with special messages. Hosea named his children Lo-ruhamah and Lo-ammi. Lo-ruhamah means "not loved," and Lo-Ammi means "not my people." By giving his children these unusual names, Hosea was giving God's message to the people. But usually names from other countries and cultures sound strange to us because we're not used to them. Names may sound funny to us, but not to the people in that country. Your name would probably sound funny to the people of Israel.

KEY VERSES: *Soon Gomer had another child. This one was a daughter. And God said to Hosea, "Name her Lo-ruhamah. This means 'No more mercy.' For I will have no more mercy upon Israel. I will not forgive her again. But I will have mercy on the tribe of Judah. I will free her from her enemies. I will do so without any help from her armies or weapons." Once Lo-ruhamah was no longer a baby, Gomer gave birth to a son. And God said, "Call him Lo-ammi. This means 'Not my people.' For Israel is not mine, and I am not her God." (Hosea 1:6-9)*

RELATED VERSES: *Genesis 30:8; 1 Samuel 25:25; Isaiah 8:1-4; Matthew 1:21*

Q: DOES SATAN KNOW ABOUT THE BIBLE?

101

A: Satan knows all about the Bible. He even knows what it says. But Satan certainly doesn't follow what the Bible teaches. In fact, he does everything he can to stop people from obeying God's Word. Just because someone knows the truth doesn't mean that he or she will do it. Satan is a liar, the father of lies. He has lied and twisted the truth so much that he has fooled himself into thinking that what the Bible predicts won't happen. Satan thinks that he can beat God and escape his punishment. But the Bible tells the truth. Eventually God will totally wipe out Satan and his demons.

KEY VERSES: *Are there still some among you who hold that "only believing" is enough? Is believing in one God enough? Well, remember that the demons believe this. And they shake with fear! Fool! Don't you know that "believing" is useless unless you do what God wants? Faith that does not result in good deeds is not real faith. (James 2:19-20)*

RELATED VERSES: *Matthew 4:6; John 5:39-40*

RELATED QUESTION: *If Satan knows the Bible, why doesn't he believe it?*

Q: WHAT IS A BIBLE?

102

A: The Bible is God's message to us. Actually, the Bible is not just one book, but a collection of many books that have been put together. It came to be called *the* Book because it is so important, because it is *God's* book. (The word *Bible* means *book*.) The Bible serves as an instruction manual for living God's way; it tells us what's right and what's wrong. It has many stories and lessons that he wants us to know. The Bible tells us about God and Jesus and how we are supposed to live. You can look in the Bible to find out what God wants you to do.

KEY VERSE: *Your words are a lamp to light the path ahead of me. They keep me from stumbling and falling. (Psalm 119:105)*

RELATED VERSES: *2 Timothy 3:16-17; 2 Peter 1:16-21*

RELATED QUESTIONS: *What does the word **Bible** mean? Why are there sixty-six books? Why would God want to invent a Bible?*

Q: DID THE BIBLE STORIES REALLY HAPPEN, OR ARE THEY LIKE FAIRY TALES?

103

A: The stories in the Bible really happened. Some of the events seem amazing to us because they're miracles, but they still happened. We know that the stories are true because the Bible is God's Word, and God wouldn't lie to us or fool us. The Bible also says that every word in it is true. Some people don't believe the Bible because they haven't read it. Some don't believe it because they don't think miracles can happen. Others don't believe because they don't want to; they don't want to learn about God and do what he tells them to do. But we know that God can do anything, and he's the best one to tell us how to live. We should pray for those who don't believe the Bible or who think it's full of fairy tales.

KEY VERSE: *All these things happened to them as examples to us. They warn us not to do the same things. They were written so we could learn from them as the world nears its end. (1 Corinthians 10:11)*

RELATED VERSES: *Luke 1:1-4; John 20:29; 21:24-25; 1 John 1:1-4*

RELATED QUESTIONS: *How do we know that what the Bible says is true? How do we know the Bible stories are true? Why do some people think the Bible isn't real? Why don't some people believe the Bible? Are the stories about Jesus true?*

NOTE TO PARENTS: *This question presents a good opportunity to take out a Bible and look at it together.*

Q: WHEN WAS THE BIBLE MADE?

104

A: God wrote the Bible over many, many years, a long time ago—long before computers, cars, and even before books. The people who wrote down God's words used scrolls of paper made from papyrus leaves and animal skin. They wrote it over a period of 1,500 years, from the time of Moses to the apostle John. Even though the Bible was written hundreds of years before we were born, it is still up-to-date. When we read the stories and understand what God is saying, we learn how we should live today.

KEY VERSES: *Long ago God spoke in many different ways to our fathers. He spoke through the prophets in visions, dreams, and even face to face. Little by little he told them about his plans. But now in these days he has spoken to us through his Son. He has given his Son everything. Through his Son he made the world and everything there is. (Hebrews 1:1-2)*

RELATED VERSES: *2 Peter 1:16-21*

RELATED QUESTIONS: *Why didn't Jesus write the Bible for us? Why did God get Moses to write part of the Bible? Why did Moses only write five Bible books?*

Q: HOW MANY PEOPLE WROTE THE BIBLE?

105

A: God used many people to write the Bible. Moses, King David, and the apostle Paul wrote a lot. God also used prophets to write down his words—Isaiah, Jeremiah, and Ezekiel, to name a few. We also know that God used many different kinds of people—old, young, kings, apostles—with many different backgrounds and personalities. God used a lot of people to write the Bible because the events described in it took place over many, many years.

KEY VERSES: *No prophecy in the Bible was thought up by the prophet himself. The Holy Spirit within these godly men gave them true messages from God. (2 Peter 1:20-21)*

RELATED VERSES: *Jeremiah 36:2; Hebrews 1:1; 2 Peter 3:16*

RELATED QUESTION: *Why did God get so many people to write the Bible?*

WHAT DOES INSPIRED MEAN?

106

A: *Inspired* describes the way God used the Bible writers to write down what he wanted them to write. (It doesn't mean "perspired.") It doesn't mean dictated; that is, God didn't say the words out loud while the writers copied them down. Inspired means that God guided the writers, helping them to write everything he wanted them to write, so that all the words in the Bible would tell us what we need to know. He gave the writers the ideas and the desire to write; then he guided them so that every word they wrote was what he wanted.

KEY VERSE: *The whole Bible was given to us by inspiration from God. It is useful to teach us what is true. It helps us to know what is wrong in our lives. It straightens us out and helps us do what is right. (2 Timothy 3:16)*

RELATED VERSES: *2 Peter 1:16-21*

RELATED QUESTIONS: *Who wrote the Bible—God or his followers? Why do we say the Bible is God's Word? How do we know that God wrote the Bible?*

Q: WHY ARE THERE FOUR BOOKS ABOUT JESUS IN THE BIBLE?

107

A: The Gospels are the books in the Bible that tell us about Jesus' birth, life, death, and resurrection. God used *four* books because each book tells the story of Jesus from a unique point of view. Each one shows us something different about Jesus. When we read all the Gospels, we see the whole picture. It's like seeing a house from all four sides.

The four stories about Jesus are all named after their writers: Matthew, Mark, Luke, and John. Matthew and John knew Jesus, went places with him, and were his close friends; they were two of Jesus' original twelve disciples. Matthew was a tax collector; Mark was a friend of the twelve disciples; Luke was a doctor; John was a fisherman.

KEY VERSE: *Jesus did many other things as well that aren't recorded here. And if all of them were written down, the whole world wouldn't hold all the books! (John 21:25)*

RELATED VERSES: *Luke 1:1-4; John 20:30-31; 21:24-25*

RELATED QUESTION: *Who wrote Matthew, Mark, Luke, and John?*

NOTE TO PARENTS: *If this question arises, open your Bible and show your kids where the four Gospels are.*

Q: WHERE DID THEY GET THE SCROLLS FROM?

108

A: Today, we use pencils and pens to write, and we write on paper. But the Bible was written a long time ago, long before these things were invented. Instead of using paper, people would write on long strips of *papyrus* or *parchment*. Papyrus was made from a plant that grows in Bible lands. Parchment was made from animal skins. Both papyrus and parchment could be sewn together and rolled up into long scrolls. Museums have some of these ancient scrolls. People read from these scrolls like books. But there weren't a lot of them because each one had to be copied by hand. Today, everyone can have his or her own Bible to read. But in those days, most synagogues and churches would only have one copy each. So the scrolls were very valuable, and the priests took good care of them. We should take care of our Bibles, too.

KEY VERSE: *When you come, bring the coat I left at Troas with Carpus. Also bring the books, but especially bring the parchments. (2 Timothy 4:13)*

RELATED VERSE: *Jeremiah 36:2*

RELATED QUESTION: *Where did they get the Bible?*

Q: IF LOTS OF DIFFERENT PEOPLE IN DIFFERENT PLACES WROTE THE BIBLE, HOW DID IT GET TOGETHER IN ONE BIG BOOK?

109

A: The first books of the Bible, the Old Testament, were written to the Jewish people. The Jews took care of and protected these books and spent countless hours carefully copying them again and again. Jesus often quoted from the Old Testament and said it was all true and that it was the Word of God. The books that we find in the New Testament were written by people who had seen Jesus or who were close to those who had contact with Jesus. Their stories about Jesus (the Gospels) and their letters (the Epistles) were read in the local churches. Church leaders collected the writings and guarded them carefully. For nearly 2,000 years now, all these Bible books have been together.

KEY VERSE: *Yes, being a Jew is good. First of all, God trusted them with his laws. That way they could know and do his will. (Romans 3:2)*

RELATED VERSES: *Matthew 5:17-20; Mark 14:49; Luke 24:27-46; John 2:22; 5:39; 7:38-42; 10:35; 17:12*

RELATED QUESTION: *What happened to the letters that Paul wrote to the churches?*

Q: WHY CAN'T WE PUT NEW BOOKS IN THE BIBLE?

110

A:

We can't put new books in the Bible because the Bible is *God's* message, not ours. It contains his words, which he inspired his people to write in a special way. Some people have tried to put new books in the Bible, but others who recognized that the Bible is a special book kept them from changing it. The story about how God has saved us is complete. God has already told us all we need to know and do.

KEY VERSE: *I have serious words for everyone who reads this book: Don't add anything to what is written here. If you do, God will give you the plagues described in this book. (Revelation 22:18)*

RELATED VERSES: *Hebrews 1:1-2*

RELATED QUESTIONS: *What if God tells someone to put new books in the Bible? What was wrong with the books that didn't make it into the Bible?*

NOTE TO PARENTS: *While Protestants and Catholics differ on the question of including the intertestamental books in the Bible, no Christian denomination is arguing for new books to be added to the Bible. Many heretical teachers and leaders have tried to add their words to those of Scripture. Many others have tried to give additional writings the same status as the books of the Bible. But God's people recognize that the Bible contains God's words, not our own, so it's not up to us what goes in it.*

Q: WILL PEOPLE WRITE ABOUT US IN A SPECIAL BIBLE, TOO?

111

A: There is only one Bible (or "revelation from God"), and it has already been written. But remember, the Bible is far more than a collection of stories about people who lived a long time ago—it's God's message about Jesus; it tells how we should live today. The Bible also tells us about the future, not just the past. So in one sense, we *are* in the Bible. We are important in God's plan. Also, the Bible tells us that those who believe in Jesus have their names written in the "Lamb's Book of Life"—that's another book that God has. It tells who will live with God in heaven.

KEY VERSE: *Nothing evil will be allowed into it. No one immoral or dishonest can be there. Only those who are written in the Lamb's Book of Life can enter the city. (Revelation 21:27)*

RELATED VERSES: *Psalm 119:129-133, 137-140*

RELATED QUESTION: *Why wasn't there a Bible written from the end of our Bible to now?*

Q: WHY DO SO MANY PEOPLE KEEP TRANSLATING THE BIBLE?

112

A: The Old Testament first was written in the Hebrew language, and the New Testament was written in Greek. If no one had ever translated the Bible, only people who could read ancient Hebrew and Greek would be able to understand the Bible today. Fortunately, over the years men and women have taken the time to put the Bible into other languages, including English, so that speakers of almost *all* languages can read it.

But some people still don't have the Bible in their own language—some don't even have a written language. For them to read God's Word, somebody has to put their language into written words. Then someone has to translate the Bible into their language so they can read it. Imagine if there were no Bibles in your language— how would you read it? God wants us to take the message about Jesus to everyone all over the world, and that means translating the Bible into every language there is. That's why people keep translating the Bible.

KEY VERSES: *"So now go and make disciples in all the nations. Baptize them into the name of the Father, the Son, and the Holy Spirit. Then teach these new disciples to obey all the commands I have given you. And be sure of this thing! I am with you always, even to the end of the world." (Matthew 28:19-20)*

RELATED VERSES: *Isaiah 6:8; 1 Timothy 4:13*

Q: WHY ISN'T THERE JUST ONE KIND OF BIBLE?

113

A: There are many kinds of Bibles because there are many kinds of people. But they all contain the same message. Different Bibles meet different needs. Some Bibles are very small so you can carry them with you. Others are big so you can see the words better. Some Bibles use everyday words to make the Bible easy to read and the lessons easy to learn. Some Bibles have notes, maps, and charts to help people understand the parts that are different from today. The purpose of all these different Bibles is to help people understand what God is saying so they can obey him.

KEY VERSE: *Until I get there, read and explain the Bible to the church. Preach God's Word. (1 Timothy 4:13)*

RELATED VERSES: *2 Timothy 2:15-16*

RELATED QUESTIONS: *Why doesn't the King James Version have the English that we speak in it? Why are some Bibles study Bibles and some aren't?*

NOTE TO PARENTS: *It is very important for children to have a translation of the Bible that they can read and understand themselves. If they ask this question because they can't understand their own Bible, consider getting them a translation that they can understand.*

Q: WHAT IS A LIVING BIBLE?

114

A: *The Living Bible* is an English version of the Bible. The words and sentences in *The Living Bible* reflect the way people speak today so that most people can understand them. The Bible talks about the Scriptures as being "living and active," so that's where the name came from. There are many other English translations of the Bible. Some of the most well-known are: the New International Version, the *New American Standard Bible,* the King James Version, the New King James Version, and the New Revised Standard Version.

KEY VERSE: *For whatever God says to us is full of living power. It is sharper than the sharpest sword. It cuts swift and deep into our innermost thoughts and desires. It shows us for what we really are. (Hebrews 4:12)*

RELATED QUESTIONS: *Why do they call **The Living Bible** the Living Bible? Is the New King James written by a new guy named King James? Is NIV the last name of the man who wrote the Bible?*

Q: WHY DID GOD PUT SCARY STORIES IN THE BIBLE?

115

A: The Bible tells true stories about real people who actually lived and died. Sometimes those stories can seem scary to us. God included those stories because he wanted to teach us something from them. That is, they weren't put there to scare us but to serve as a warning of what to avoid, to show us what we should do, and to help us learn how to live. Some teachings in the Bible seem scary to people, especially people who disobey God, because the stories reveal the bad that can happen when we choose to do evil. Hopefully, these teachings will show us how important it is to listen to God.

KEY VERSE: *All these things happened to them as examples to us. They warn us not to do the same things. They were written so we could learn from them as the world nears its end. (1 Corinthians 10:11)*

RELATED VERSES: *Psalm 119:105; John 20:30-31; Revelation 1:3*

RELATED QUESTION: *Why did God tell us about all sorts of terrible things that happen?*

Q: IS ARCHAEOLOGY THE STUDY OF NOAH'S ARK?

116

A: Archaeology is the study of ancient cultures. It tells us about Bible times and people who lived long ago and what life was like back then. Archaeologists are the people who study and teach about archaeology. They find out about Bible times by digging up old cities to find buildings and things people used long ago. They are even trying to find Noah's ark. Archaeologists study other places, too, and have shown us many interesting things about people and places all over the world.

KEY VERSES: *So the flood slowly went away. And 150 days after it began, the boat came to rest upon the mountains of Ararat. (Genesis 8:3-4)*

RELATED VERSES: *Genesis 6:9–8:22*

RELATED QUESTIONS: *What is archaeology? How do we know about Bible times? Have they found Noah's ark yet?*

Q: WHY DO WE STUDY THE BIBLE?

117

A: It's important to study the Bible because the Bible is God's message to us and studying it helps us know and understand it better. If you want to learn more about butterflies, you study butterflies. Studying the Bible helps us find out how to live and to find out what God wants. When we only read the Bible (without studying it), we may not see the meaning right away. *Studying* helps us learn lessons for life—we learn God's will so we can obey him. Studying the Bible is like reading a story many, many times—each time you see something different and learn more.

KEY VERSE: *Work hard so God can say to you, "Well done." Be a good workman. Then you won't be ashamed when God examines your work. Know what his Word says and means. (2 Timothy 2:15)*

RELATED VERSES: *2 Timothy 3:16-17*

RELATED QUESTIONS: *How come God makes us do homework? What's doctrine? What's theology? Why do people have different ways of understanding the Bible?*

Q: HOW CAN KIDS STUDY THE BIBLE?

118

A: Studying the Bible is not as difficult as it may sound. In fact, it can be fun! First, start out by just reading the Bible. Read short portions—a paragraph or story—and read it in a translation you understand. Second, ask a parent to explain big words to you that you don't understand. Third, memorize verses that tell you what you should do. As you read and study, you will have questions about what the Bible means. Save your questions and find someone to answer them, like a parent, teacher, or pastor. It's good to read the Bible every day. Make it a habit. And if you get really ambitious, you can use a Bible dictionary and atlas; a dictionary tells what Bible words mean, and an atlas shows where Bible places are.

KEY VERSE: *"Always remind the people about these laws. You yourself must think about them every day and every night. That way you will be sure to obey all of them. For only then will you succeed." (Joshua 1:8)*

RELATED VERSES: *Deuteronomy 6:6-9; Joshua 1:6-8; Psalm 119:1-176; Proverbs 1:1-9*

RELATED QUESTIONS: *Should we study the Bible every day? Why does God want us to do homework? What's a running reference?*

NOTE TO PARENTS: *A child asking this question may provide a good opportunity to introduce him or her to study. Get out a Bible and start a study together. Some Bible books that many kids will find interesting include Genesis, Mark, Romans, and James. If you are unfamiliar with the Bible, you can use this book to help you get an overview.*

Q: WHAT'S A CONCORDANCE?

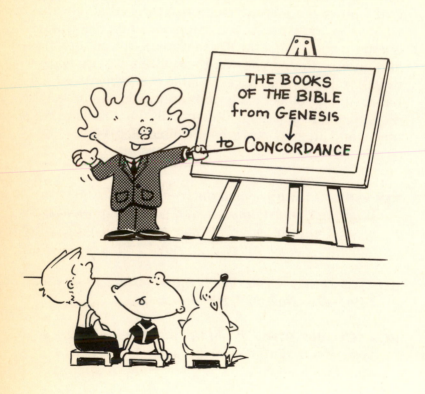

119

A: A concordance is an index of words in the Bible. It lists the words that appear in the Bible and all the verses where those words appear. Many study Bibles include a concordance in the back. If you know part of a verse but don't know where to find it in the Bible, you can look up one of the verse's words in the concordance, and it'll tell you where the word is used. For example, if you want to find the verse, "God loved the world so much that he gave his only Son. Anyone who believes in him will not die but have eternal life," you could look up the word *believes* in the concordance. It would tell you all the places where *believes* is used, and you could see if any of them is the one you're looking for. For practice, see if you can find it now!

KEY VERSE: *Work hard so God can say to you, "Well done." Be a good workman. Then you won't be ashamed when God examines your work. Know what his Word says and means. (2 Timothy 2:15)*

RELATED QUESTION: *Why does Daddy use big books to study the Bible?*

Q: WHY DO WE MEMORIZE VERSES?

120

A: We memorize Bible verses because we want to remember what God has told us. When we have the Bible in our head, God's Word will be with us when we're out playing, at the pool, or doing anything—it's with us wherever we go. Then, when we face a problem or a tough situation, we will be able to remember what God has told us to do. It's also fun to memorize verses—then during the day, we can think about the verses and what they mean.

KEY VERSE: *Your words are a lamp to light the path ahead of me. They keep me from stumbling and falling. (Psalm 119:105)*

RELATED VERSES: *Psalm 119:11; 2 Timothy 2:15*

RELATED QUESTIONS: *Can we memorize the whole Bible? How can we memorize the whole Bible? What does meditating on the Bible mean?*

NOTE TO PARENTS: *Don't make Bible memorization feel like a chore, and never use it as a punishment for bad behavior. Instead, make it into a game. The goal is for children to **enjoy** reading the Bible and memorizing verses, not merely that they have a lot of Bible knowledge. Some good ones to start with include John 3:16, Genesis 1:1, and Romans 12:9.*

121

A: The Bible has two main parts: the Old Testament and the New Testament. The Old Testament tells the story of the beginning of the world and the beginning of the nation of Israel. It also tells about how the people of Israel obeyed and disobeyed God over many, many years. All of the stories and messages from God in the Old Testament lead up to Jesus Christ. The New Testament tells the story of Christ, the early Christians, and the future. You can think of the Old Testament and New Testament as "before Christ" and "after Christ," or as volume 1 and volume 2. Old doesn't mean out-of-date—it means that it happened before Jesus. But remember, even though the Bible has two main parts, it is all one book—God's book.

KEY VERSE: *"You search the Scriptures, for you believe they give you eternal life. And the Scriptures point to me!" (John 5:39)*

RELATED VERSES: *John 10:35; 2 Timothy 3:14-15; Hebrews 1:1-2*

RELATED QUESTIONS: *Why is one called **old** and one called **new**? What is the Old Testament?*

NOTE TO PARENTS: *If your kids aren't already familiar with the two parts, pick up a Bible and show them the Old Testament and New Testament.*

Q: WHAT IS THE BIBLE'S BIGGEST STORY?

122

A: The Bible's biggest story is the story of Jesus. In fact, the whole Bible tells his story—about God creating people and saving them from sin. Jesus came to the world to die in our place, to pay the penalty for our sins. If we trust in Christ as Savior, God gives us eternal life. The Old Testament Bible writers told us that Jesus would be born, live, die, and rise again. Even the sacrifices described in the book of Leviticus show us what the death of Christ would be, the perfect "Lamb of God who takes away the sin of the world." No matter where you look in the Bible, you can learn about Jesus. Have you put your faith in him?

KEY VERSE: *"God loved the world so much that he gave his only Son. Anyone who believes in him will not die but have eternal life." (John 3:16)*

RELATED VERSES: *John 5:39; 20:31; Acts 4:12*

NOTE TO PARENTS: *The Bible's biggest story is also a parent's biggest responsibility. In order to be ready for the day when a child asks a question like this one, plan what you will say and which Scriptures you will use to introduce him or her to Jesus.*

OLD
TESTAMENT
EVENTS
AND
PEOPLE

Q: HOW DID GOD MAKE PEOPLE?

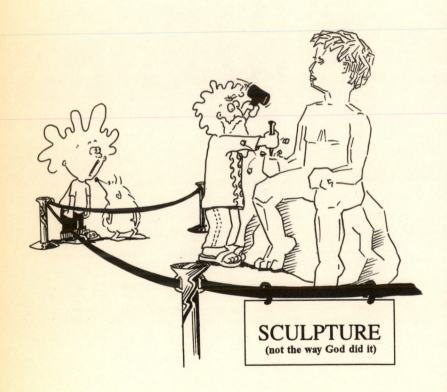

SCULPTURE
(not the way God did it)

123

A: The Bible tells us that God made Adam from the "dust of the ground." In other words, God took something he had already made, dust, and formed a man's body out of it and then gave that body life. God made Adam, the first man, just the way he wanted him. Then God made Eve from part of Adam, just the way he wanted her. We're all made by God. And he has made us just right.

KEY VERSE: *The time came when the Lord God formed a man's body. He made it from the dust of the ground. Then he breathed into it the breath of life. And man became a living person. (Genesis 2:7)*

RELATED VERSES: *Genesis 1:26-27; 2:21-22*

RELATED QUESTIONS: *How come God made Eve out of Adam's rib? What did God use to make people? Why did God only make people on earth and not on other planets? Why didn't God make the woman out of dust?*

Q: IF ADAM AND EVE HADN'T SINNED, WOULD PEOPLE SIN TODAY?

124

A: We really don't know what would have happened if Adam and Eve hadn't sinned in the Garden of Eden, but their temptation was a very important test. Unfortunately, they failed the test, and sin entered the world; the perfect world became damaged, broken, and dirty. Because of Adam and Eve's sin, every person who has ever lived has been born a sinner. Sin is passed on from parents to their children. We do wrong things because we're sinners.

KEY VERSE: *Adam caused many to be sinners because he disobeyed God. Christ caused many to be welcome to God because he obeyed. (Romans 5:19)*

RELATED VERSES: *Romans 5:12-19*

RELATED QUESTION: *Would Satan still be here on earth trying to get people to be evil if Adam and Eve hadn't sinned?*

NOTE TO PARENTS: *Though Adam and Eve sinned, God made a way for all people to come back to him—to be forgiven—by sending Jesus.*

Q: WHAT MADE THE GARDEN OF EDEN PRETTIER THAN OTHER GARDENS TODAY?

125

A: The Garden of Eden was more beautiful than any garden today because God made it that way. Eden was perfect, and God was there. The whole world was perfect because it hadn't yet been spoiled by sin. When Adam and Eve sinned, God made them leave the Garden, and the whole world changed because of their sin. Thistles and thorns began to grow, animals began to eat each other, and human beings had to work hard at living in the world.

KEY VERSE: *So the Lord God sent him away from the Garden of Eden forever. He sent him out to farm the ground from which he had been taken. (Genesis 3:23)*

RELATED VERSES: *Genesis 3:17-19, 22-24; Isaiah 55:12-13; Romans 8:22*

RELATED QUESTIONS: *Why did Adam and Eve leave the Garden? Why wouldn't the angels let Adam and Eve into the Garden of Eden? Why were Adam and Eve naked?*

Q: WHY DID EVE DISOBEY GOD WHEN SHE KNEW SHE WOULD DIE?

126

A: Eve disobeyed God because Satan *deceived* her. That is, the devil used lies and tricks to get her to disobey God. God had said that Adam and Eve would die if they ate of the "Tree of Conscience," but Satan said they wouldn't. Because Eve believed Satan, she wasn't sure what would happen. Another trick Satan used was to promise that it would do great things for her; he said that if she ate the forbidden fruit, she would be as God. That sounded good to Eve, and so she did what Satan suggested. Temptation tells you that feeling good right now is better than anything that might happen in the future. Satan still deceives people by twisting God's words and making people believe lies.

Satan wants us to think that once we sin, God can't forgive us. But even though Eve sinned, and even though we sin, God had a plan for taking away our sin. That plan was to send Jesus.

KEY VERSE: *"For you are the children of your father the devil. You love to do the evil things he does. He was a murderer from the beginning. There was no truth in him. When he lies, it is perfectly normal. For he is the father of lies."* *(John 8:44)*

RELATED VERSES: *Genesis 2:16-17; 3:1-5; Matthew 6:13; 26:41; 2 Corinthians 2:11*

RELATED QUESTIONS: *Did God want Eve to be deceived and eat of the fruit? Does God still love Adam and Eve?*

Q: WHY DID CAIN KILL HIS BROTHER?

127

A: The story of Cain and Abel shows the effects of sin in the world. The first sin was when Adam and Eve disobeyed God and ate from the Tree of Conscience. After that, every person has been born a sinner, someone who will often do what's wrong instead of what's right. Cain's sins of jealousy and hatred led to murder. Both Cain and Abel had presented gifts to God, but Abel's gifts had pleased God, while Cain's had not. Cain became jealous of God's favor; this made Cain very angry (Genesis 4:5). Cain's jealousy and anger led him to kill his brother. We can see from this story that jealousy and anger can cause people to do terrible harm, even to people they love. Watch out for those feelings, and take care of them before they hurt you, too!

KEY VERSE: *We are not to be like Cain. He belonged to Satan and killed his brother. Why did he kill him? Because Cain had been doing wrong. He knew very well that his brother's life was better than his. (1 John 3:12)*

RELATED VERSES: *Genesis 4:1-16; Matthew 5:21-24; Hebrews 11:4*

RELATED QUESTION: *Why did Cain and Abel fight?*

Q: HOW DID NOAH BUILD A BOAT THAT WAS SO BIG?

128

A: We don't know exactly *how* Noah built the huge boat (which we call the "ark"). But God told him what size to make it and what materials to use, and Noah obeyed God's instructions to the letter. The boat had to be very large because it would have to hold Noah, his children, their families, and hundreds of animals. It had to be a boat because God was going to flood the whole earth. It took a long time for Noah to build the boat. He probably used his whole family in the building project.

Why did Noah build the ark? Because everyone in the whole world had become so evil and violent, God was going to kill everyone with a flood. Noah was the only good man in the world, so he and his family would survive in the boat. And all the animals Noah brought on the ark would survive, too. Noah did everything God told him—he obeyed God.

KEY VERSE: *And Noah did all that God told him. (Genesis 6:22)*

RELATED VERSES: *Genesis 6:11-22; Hebrews 11:7*

RELATED QUESTIONS: *Why did Noah build a boat? Did God get into the ark before he shut the door? How did Noah get the animals from all over the earth? How did Noah gather all the animals on the ark?*

Q: WHY DID GOD FLOOD THE WHOLE EARTH?

129

A: God made the rain fall and the water rise in order to flood the whole earth so that all the evil people in the world would drown. Because of sin, the world had gotten worse and worse. It was so bad that God became very sad; God was even sorry that he had created human beings. People were evil, mean, cruel, and violent. God gave them 120 years to improve; they had many chances to obey God, but they only got worse. Only Noah and his family were trying to live God's way (only one family in the whole world!). Noah tried to tell people about God, but no one would listen. So God decided to destroy all the human beings, except Noah and his family.

KEY VERSE: *Meanwhile, the crime rate was rising rapidly across the earth. As seen by God, the world was rotten to the core. (Genesis 6:11)*

RELATED VERSES: *Genesis 6:11-13; Hebrews 11:7; 2 Peter 2:5*

RELATED QUESTIONS: *Why were all the other people bad? Was there not even one other Christian on the land anywhere in the world other than Noah? When the Flood came, did the people who could swim die too? Did fish die in the Flood?*

Q: WHY DID GOD PUT A RAINBOW IN THE SKY?

130

A: After the rains stopped, the flood waters went down, and Noah, his family, and the animals left the ark, God promised that he would never again send a flood to destroy the earth. Then God put a rainbow in the clouds as a sign of this promise. Whenever we see a rainbow, it reminds us of the Flood, the reason for it, and God's promise never to flood the earth again.

KEY VERSES: *"I will never again send another flood to destroy the earth. And I seal my promise with this sign. I have placed my rainbow in the clouds. It is a sign of my promise until the end of time, to you and to all the earth." (Genesis 9:11-13)*

RELATED VERSES: *Genesis 9:12-17*

RELATED QUESTIONS: *Did it ever rain before the Flood? Why did God give Noah a rainbow?*

NOTE TO PARENTS: *God gives us symbols and images to remind us of his love and promises. The cross, for example, reminds us of Christ's death for us. The empty tomb reminds us of his power over sin and death. His throne in heaven reminds us of his authority.*

Q: WHY DID GOD CHOOSE ABRAHAM TO GO TO THE PROMISED LAND INSTEAD OF SOMEONE ELSE?

DEAR GOD please choose me

131

A: God chose Abraham (called Abram at first) to go to the Promised Land (which would later be called Israel) and to become the father of a great nation. Abraham was chosen, not because he was especially good, but simply because God wanted him—the Bible doesn't give us God's reasons. God doesn't always tell us why he does what he does. God knows everything and can do anything he wants. God knew that Abraham would obey.

KEY VERSES: *God had told Abram, "Leave your own country behind you, and your own people. Go to the land I will guide you to. If you do, I will cause you to become the father of a great nation. I will bless you and make your name famous. You will be a blessing to many others." (Genesis 12:1-2)*

RELATED VERSES: *Genesis 12:1-3; Hebrews 11:8-10*

RELATED QUESTIONS: *Why did God tell Abraham to go away from his home? Did God choose Abraham because he was the best person in the world?*

Q: WHY WAS ABRAHAM WILLING TO KILL HIS OWN SON?

132

A: One day God told Abraham to take his son, Isaac, up into the mountains and offer him as a sacrifice. Abraham took the trip and was willing to kill his own son because he knew that he had to obey God. Isaac was a miracle child, a special gift from God, and Abraham loved him very much. It was *very difficult* for Abraham to take Isaac and prepare him to be killed. But Abraham loved and obeyed God; he had faith and expected a miracle. Abraham believed that God could and would raise Isaac from the dead. This request from God was a test of Abraham's faith. Abraham believed that God's plan wouldn't be stopped. The good news, of course, is that Abraham didn't have to kill Isaac—God provided an animal to be sacrificed instead. Many years later, God sacrificed his own Son, Jesus, for us.

KEY VERSE: *[Abraham] believed that if Isaac died God would bring him back to life. That is just about what happened. As far as Abraham knew, Isaac was doomed to death. But he came back again, alive! (Hebrews 11:19)*

RELATED VERSES: *Genesis 22:1-19; Hebrews 11:17-19*

RELATED QUESTIONS: *If Abraham sacrificing his son was like God sacrificing Jesus, then why didn't God stop the people just before they killed Jesus? Why was it important for Abraham to have a son?*

Q: **WHY DID JACOB TRICK HIS DAD?**

133

A: Isaac had two sons, Jacob and Esau. Jacob tricked his father because he wanted the inheritance that should have gone to his brother. Jacob was selfish and greedy. Also, he was his mom's favorite child, and when his mother told him how to trick his father, he went along and did what she said. Although Jacob received the inheritance, his actions broke up the family and caused everyone a lot of grief.

KEY VERSES: *Rebekah: "Now do exactly as I tell you. Go out to the flocks and bring me two young goats. I will prepare your father's favorite dish from them. Then take it to your father. After he has enjoyed it he will bless you before his death, instead of Esau!" (Genesis 27:8-10)*

RELATED VERSES: *Genesis 27:1-40*

RELATED QUESTIONS: *Why did Jacob and Esau both want to be the leader? What's a birthright?*

Q: WHY DID JOSEPH'S BROTHERS SELL HIM?

134

A: Joseph had ten older brothers (and one younger brother, Benjamin). Joseph's older brothers didn't like him because Joseph was their father's favorite son. (Joseph was Jacob's favorite because Joseph was born when Jacob was an old man.) They were jealous of him. Joseph's father even gave him a special gift—a beautiful coat. Joseph also made his brothers angry because he would tell his father about some of the bad things they would do, and he would tell his older brothers about his dreams in which the brothers bowed down before him. Eventually the brothers became so upset with Joseph that they decided to kill him. But one brother, Reuben, talked the others into putting Joseph into a well instead of killing him. He planned to set Joseph free later. But while Reuben was gone, the other brothers sold him to some foreign traders as a slave.

KEY VERSES: *"Here comes that master dreamer," they said. "Come on. Let's kill him and toss him into a well. We can tell Father that a wild animal has eaten him. Then we'll see what will become of all his dreams!" (Genesis 37:19-20)*

RELATED VERSES: *Genesis 37:12-36*

RELATED QUESTIONS: *Why did Joseph's dad give him a new coat? Why did Jacob love Joseph the best?*

Q: WHY DIDN'T JOSEPH GO BACK HOME?

135

A: Joseph may have wanted to go back home (certainly he missed his father, mother, and little brother), but he couldn't—first because he was a slave, then because he was in prison, and finally because he was in government service. He also was a long way from home, and transportation was different from today; Joseph couldn't just hop on a bus or train and go home. Also, Joseph may have been afraid of facing his brothers again; remember, they had wanted to kill him and then had sold him into slavery. It's good that Joseph stayed in Egypt because God used him in his powerful position in the government to save his family (and thousands of others) from starvation. And eventually God brought the whole family back together again in Egypt with Joseph—all part of God's plan to bring Jesus to earth.

KEY VERSE: *"Yes, it was God who sent me here, not you! And he has made me a counselor to Pharaoh. I am the manager of this entire nation, ruler of all the land of Egypt." (Genesis 45:8)*

RELATED VERSES: *Genesis 41:41-57; 45:4-9*

RELATED QUESTION: *When Joseph's brothers came back to Egypt to live with him, why did they think he was still mad at them?*

Q: WHY DIDN'T THE BUSH BURN UP?

Bible Experiment #2

136

A: One day while watching sheep, a man named Moses saw a bush on fire that would not burn up. The bush didn't turn into ashes because God was present, doing a miracle to get Moses' attention. When Moses saw the bush and heard God's voice, he was ready to listen. God used the burning bush to help Moses see that God had the power to do what he said he would do—rescue the people of Israel from slavery in Egypt.

KEY VERSES: *Suddenly the Angel of the Lord appeared to [Moses] as a flame of fire in a bush. Moses saw that the bush was on fire. But it didn't burn up. So he went over to see why. Then God called out to him, "Moses! Moses!" "Who is it?" Moses asked. (Exodus 3:2-4)*

RELATED VERSES: *Exodus 3:1–4:18*

RELATED QUESTIONS: *How did God choose Moses? Did God know that Moses would be afraid to go? Was Jesus in the burning bush? How did Moses make his shepherd rod into a snake?*

Q: WHY WASN'T MOSES AFRAID TO GO TO PHARAOH?

137

A: Moses probably was afraid to go to Pharaoh, but he went anyway out of obedience to God. When God said he was going to send Moses to Pharaoh to demand that he let the Israelites go, Moses was very frightened at the idea. In fact, he tried to get out of the job by using all sorts of excuses: he said he wasn't the right person, the people would wonder why he should be the one to lead them, the people wouldn't believe that God had sent him, and he wasn't a good speaker. Finally, when Moses had run out of excuses, he simply pleaded: "Lord, please! Send someone else" (Exodus 4:13). But God wanted Moses to go, and Moses did go—God gave him strength and stayed with him. Moses was able to lead God's people out of slavery and to the Promised Land. The Bible doesn't say Moses wasn't afraid; it says he obeyed God.

KEY VERSE: *"Now I am going to send you to Pharaoh. You will demand that he let you lead my people out of Egypt."* *(Exodus 3:10)*

RELATED VERSES: *Exodus 3:7–4:17*

RELATED QUESTIONS: *Why were all the Israelites slaves except for Moses? Why would God let the magicians do the same miracles as Aaron and Moses? How did the sorcerers do the same miracles as Moses? How come Moses kept asking God to take away the plagues when he knew Pharaoh would change his mind again?*

Q: WHY WOULDN'T PHARAOH LET THE PEOPLE GO?

138

A: Pharaoh is a title, like "king." The pharaoh in charge of Egypt when Moses lived was different from the pharaoh whom Joseph served—that pharaoh was kind and generous to the Israelites. But this pharaoh was mean; he forced the Israelites to serve the Egyptians as slaves. When Moses went to see Pharaoh and asked him to let the Israelites leave Egypt to worship in the wilderness, Pharaoh was furious. He was too proud to give in to a slave, and he thought he would lose his slave labor, so he refused. Moses went back to him with the request and did special signs to prove that he had been sent by God, but Pharaoh still said no. Finally God sent a series of plagues to convince Pharaoh to let the people go. After each plague, Pharaoh would agree to let the people go, but then he would change his mind and refuse. The Lord hardened Pharaoh's heart in order to punish him and demonstrate God's power.

KEY VERSE: *"This is the finger of God," [the magicians] exclaimed to Pharaoh. But Pharaoh's heart was hard and stubborn. He wouldn't listen to them, just as the Lord had predicted. (Exodus 8:19)*

RELATED VERSES: *Exodus 5:1-9; 6:1-13; 7:1-14; 8:1–12:36*

RELATED QUESTIONS: *Why did the Lord keep hardening Pharaoh's heart? Was the pharaoh who wouldn't let the Israelites go the same one that Joseph knew?*

Q: WHY DID GOD SEND PLAGUES ON EGYPT?

139

A: God sent the plagues to Egypt to punish Pharaoh and to show God's power. The plagues were miracles—fantastic demonstrations of God's power. Pharaoh saw himself as a god, and God was showing him who the true God was. Also, God was answering the prayers of the Israelites to deliver them from slavery. The Egyptians were holding the Israelites captive and did not want to let them go. Each time Pharaoh would refuse to let the people go, God would send a plague on the Egyptians (but not the Israelites) to help convince Pharaoh to change his mind. After each plague, Pharaoh would agree to release the Israelites, but then he would harden his heart and say no. Eventually, after the death of the firstborn male children, the Israelites were allowed to leave Egypt. But even then, Pharaoh changed his mind and chased after them. Pharaoh was an evil man.

KEY VERSES: *"Go back to Pharaoh," the Lord told Moses. "Tell him, 'The Lord . . . demands that you let his people go to sacrifice to him. If you refuse, the power of God will send a deadly plague. It will destroy your cattle, horses, donkeys, camels, flocks, and herds. But the plague will affect only the cattle of Egypt. None of the Israelite herds and flocks will even be touched!'" (Exodus 9:1-4)*

RELATED VERSES: *Exodus 3:5-10; 7:14–12:33*

RELATED QUESTIONS: *Did the hail fall on the Israelites? How can darkness be felt? How could it be dark in one place and light in another? Why did Pharaoh want the Israelites to come back? Did Pharaoh get the boils as well? Did the Egyptians slaves get killed in the hail? How could the Nile river being blood have fresh water around to dig up?*

Q: WHY DID THE ISRAELITES SMEAR BLOOD ON THEIR DOORS?

140

A: The blood on the doors helped the Israelites prepare for God's final plague on Egypt. That plague would kill all the firstborn males in Egypt except those who lived in the homes marked by the blood on the doors. The blood came from a perfect lamb that they killed and ate that night. The blood showed their faith that God would do as he said and rescue them from slavery. Though the people at that time didn't know it, the blood also represented Christ's death on the cross. By trusting in Jesus, men and women and boys and girls can be rescued from slavery to sin . . . and receive *eternal* life.

KEY VERSE: *"For the Lord will pass through the land and kill the Egyptians. But he will see the blood on the panel at the top of the door and on the two side pieces. And he will pass over that home. He will not permit the Destroyer to enter and kill your firstborn." (Exodus 12:23)*

RELATED VERSES: *Exodus 12:1-36; Hebrews 11:28*

RELATED QUESTIONS: *Why did God kill the Egyptian babies? What did the Israelites take with them when they left Egypt? How come the Israelites couldn't cook their bread before they left Egypt? How come the Israelites couldn't have any lamb leftovers?*

NOTE TO PARENTS: *It is sometimes difficult for children to understand why God asked his people to sacrifice animals. Explain that God does everything for our good—God is love, and he does whatever benefits us all. He's just and kind, and his plans for us are good.*

Q: HOW DID MOSES PART THE RED SEA?

141

A: After Moses and the Israelites left Egypt, Pharaoh changed his mind and sent soldiers to bring them back. When the fleeing Israelites came to the Red Sea, it looked as if they would be caught by the soldiers because there seemed to be no way across the water. But Moses held his rod over the edge of the sea, and God made the waters part so the people could march across to the other side on dry ground. Moses himself didn't part the Red Sea—it was a miracle that God did through him. God used Moses to lead the people to safety. Once the Israelites were safe on the other side, God allowed the water to return to normal, and the Egyptian army was drowned.

KEY VERSES: *Meanwhile, Moses stretched his rod over the sea. The Lord opened up a path through the sea. There were walls of water on each side. And a strong east wind blew all that night. It dried the sea bottom. So the people of Israel walked through the sea on dry ground! (Exodus 14:21-22)*

RELATED VERSES: *Exodus 14:15-31; Hebrews 11:29*

RELATED QUESTIONS: *How did God part the Red Sea? How could God make the wheels of the chariots fall off? Why did Pharaoh want the Israelites to come back?*

Q: WHY DID GOD GIVE MOSES SO MANY LAWS FOR THE ISRAELITES TO OBEY?

A: Moses led the Israelites to Mount Sinai, where God met with Moses and gave him laws that are recorded in the book of Leviticus. When we read Leviticus, it seems as if God gave the Israelites a lot of laws to obey. Actually, today most cities and towns have far more laws than are listed in Leviticus. (The basic laws are the Ten Commandments—many of the other laws grew out of these.) Some of the laws God gave helped organize the Israelites into a nation; some helped keep the people healthy; others told them (and us) how to live. God knew what was best for the people, and he wanted what was best for them, so he gave them many instructions.

KEY VERSE: *Moses kept on speaking to the people of Israel. He said, "Listen carefully now to all these laws God has given you. Learn them, and be sure to obey them!" (Deuteronomy 5:1)*

RELATED VERSES: *Exodus 20:1-17; Deuteronomy 5:1-22; Galatians 3:24*

RELATED QUESTIONS: *Why did God give Moses only ten commandments? Why didn't the rest of the Israelites go up the mountain with Moses and talk to God?*

NOTE TO PARENTS: *The law guided the Israelites, but it also shows us that we are sinners. That is, it shows us that we can't obey perfectly. You can use this to explain how we all break God's law, making us guilty before God and in need of salvation through faith in Christ.*

Q: WHY DID THE ISRAELITES WHO LEFT EGYPT HAVE TO WANDER IN THE WILDERNESS UNTIL THEY DIED?

143

A:

Through Moses, God led the Israelites right to the Promised Land, the land he had promised to Abraham. (This is also the land that Jacob and his sons left when they went to live with Joseph in Egypt.) Moses had sent twelve spies into Canaan to see what the land and the Canaanites were like. Ten spies reported that the Canaanites were giants that the Israelites shouldn't try to fight. But Joshua and Caleb, who knew God would help them, said, "Let us go up at once and possess it! For we are well able to conquer it!" (Numbers 13:30). Unfortunately, the people listened to the report of the ten and refused to obey God and march into the land. Those Israelites never saw the Promised Land because they didn't have faith to do what God wanted them to do; they wandered in the wilderness for forty years.

KEY VERSES: *"'The spies were in the land for 40 days. Thus, you must wander in the wilderness for 40 years. You will wander a year for each day. You will bear the burden of your sins. I will teach you what it means to reject me. I, the Lord, have spoken. Every one of you who has turned against me shall die here in this wilderness.'" (Numbers 14:34-35)*

RELATED VERSES: *Numbers 13:1–14:45*

RELATED QUESTIONS: *Why did the Israelites listen to the ten unbelieving spies instead of to Joshua and Caleb? Why did Joshua only send two spies into the Promised Land instead of twelve? Why did the Israelites believe they could go into the Promised Land the second time when they didn't believe the first time?*

Q: DID THE ISRAELITES HAVE LAWYERS AND COURTS FOR THEIR JUDGES?

144

A: Joshua was the Israelites' leader when they first got to the Promised Land. After Joshua died, God used judges to lead his people. The judges that we read about in the book of Judges were not like the judges we have today, so they didn't have courts or listen to lawyers. The Israelite judges were their nation's spiritual leaders and sometimes military leaders. Their main job was to organize the people, rescue them from enemies, and lead the people to God. This was how God led the Israelites, much the way parents lead their children.

KEY VERSE: *The Lord raised up judges. They were chosen to save the Israelites from their enemies. (Judges 2:16)*

RELATED VERSES: *Judges 2:16-23; 1 Samuel 8:1-22*

RELATED QUESTION: *What is a judge?*

Q: WAS SAMSON A GOOD GUY OR A BAD GUY?

145

A: One of Israel's judges was a man named Samson. Samson served God and wanted to please him, but he wasn't perfect. God had chosen him to do a special service for the nation of Israel—to rescue his people from cruel enemies. Samson fulfilled that job well. But Samson also did some cruel and foolish things, just as most people do. God didn't force him to do everything right. Like us, Samson had the freedom to choose to use his God-given abilities (in his case, strength) for good or bad. Sometimes Samson chose to go his own way instead of God's.

KEY VERSE: *"Your son's hair must never be cut. For he shall be a Nazirite. He shall be a special servant of God from the day he is born. And he will begin to rescue Israel from the Philistines." (Judges 13:5)*

RELATED VERSES: *Judges 13:1–16:31*

RELATED QUESTION: *Why did the Philistines want to capture Samson?*

Q: WHY DID SAMSON TELL DELILAH HIS SECRET?

146

A: Samson was in love with a woman named Delilah even though Delilah did not really love him and was a friend of his enemies. When some of those enemies offered her money to help them capture Samson, Delilah agreed and asked him for the secret of his strength. At first he gave her the wrong answers, but she nagged him and prodded him until finally Samson told her the truth—his strength came from God as part of a vow that included not cutting his hair. He told her that if his hair were cut, the Lord and his strength would leave him. Samson let himself be tricked because he was blinded by his feelings for Delilah. We need to be careful about our friends; even people we care about and like may sometimes want us to do bad things. Whenever that happens, we should obey God.

KEY VERSES: *She nagged at him every day until he couldn't stand it any longer. In the end, he told her his secret. "My hair has never been cut," he confessed. "For I've been a Nazirite to God since before my birth. If my hair were cut, my strength would leave me. I would become as weak as anyone else." (Judges 16:16-17)*

RELATED VERSES: *Judges 16:1-22*

RELATED QUESTIONS: *How did Samson get his strength? When Delilah kept asking Samson about what his secret was, why did he tell her when he knew she would tell the Philistines?*

Q: WHY DID HANNAH LEAVE HER SON AT THE CHURCH?

147

A:

For a long time, Hannah was unable to have children, and that bothered her very much. One day, while crying and praying to God, she vowed that if God would answer her prayer and give her a son, she would give the boy back to God, dedicating his life to serving God. When Samuel was born, Hannah remembered her promise to God; a few years later, when Samuel was old enough to eat solid food, she brought Samuel to the tabernacle (the place where God's people worshiped). Leaving Samuel there was like leaving him at a boarding school, with people who would love and care for him and teach him God's ways. Hannah wasn't abandoning Samuel; she was leaving him with teachers who would train him to become a priest and servant of God. Hannah's son was in good hands. Samuel grew up to be a leader of Israel and a spokesman for God.

KEY VERSES: *"I asked [God] to give me this child. And he has given me what I asked for! Now I am giving him to the Lord for as long as he lives." So [Hannah] left him there at the Tabernacle for the Lord to use. (1 Samuel 1:27-28)*

RELATED VERSES: *1 Samuel 1:1-28; 2:20-21*

RELATED QUESTION: *Why did God choose Samuel instead of a grown-up or someone who knew him better?*

NOTE TO PARENTS: *Questions like this one may have others hidden underneath: Will I be left alone with strangers? Does God think it's good for children to be left with strangers? Do my parents care about me? Be sensitive to this concern and reassure your children of God's care and your commitment to love and nurture them.*

Q: WHY DID THE PEOPLE WANT TO HAVE A KING?

148

A: The people of Israel were unhappy with God as their king and wanted to be like all the other nations—to have a human king who would lead them in battle. Times were tough, and Samuel's sons were turning out to be bad judges. They were accepting bribes and making wrong decisions. Samuel knew that God wanted the people to trust in God and not in a king, but God told Samuel to give them one anyway, along with a warning that a king would bring them many hardships. The man chosen to be Israel's first king was Saul; he was tall and handsome, but very shy. Saul started out to be a good king, but then became bad because he disobeyed God.

KEY VERSE: *"Do as they say," the Lord replied. "For I am the one they are rejecting, not you. They do not want me to be their king any longer." (1 Samuel 8:7)*

RELATED VERSES: *1 Samuel 8:1-22*

RELATED QUESTIONS: *Why did Saul hide in the baggage? Was Saul a wicked man?*

Q: WHAT DID GOLIATH EAT THAT MADE HIM SO BIG?

149

A: Goliath was a very big man—over nine feet tall. If he were alive today, he would be able to dunk a basketball without jumping, and his head would touch the net. We don't know how Goliath got to be so big, but he was a giant of a man. Goliath was as nasty as he was big; he hated the Israelites and would make fun of them and God. King Saul and his soldiers were afraid of fighting him. But a young man named David wasn't afraid. He knew that he had to fight against this man who stood against God, no matter how big he was. And he knew he would win because God would fight for him.

KEY VERSE: *Then Goliath came out of the Philistine ranks to face Israel's army. He was a Philistine champion from Gath. Goliath was a giant of a man! He was over nine feet tall! (1 Samuel 17:4)*

RELATED VERSES: *1 Samuel 17:4-11*

RELATED QUESTIONS: *How tall was Goliath? How did Goliath get so tall if his mom was a regular-sized person? Was Goliath's mom a giant? How did Goliath get so big?*

Q: HOW DID DAVID FIGHT GOLIATH IF HE WAS SO SMALL?

150

A: Although David wasn't a big man or a soldier, he wasn't afraid to fight the giant Goliath because he trusted in God, not in his own strength or in a soldier's weapons and armor. In fact, he wouldn't wear the king's armor when it was offered to him. David remembered that he had defeated lions and bears while protecting his father's sheep. David also knew that he would not fight Goliath in hand-to-hand combat; instead, he would use a sling and a stone. Also, David was about sixteen, not a little boy. David trusted in God and knew that he had to fight Goliath because Goliath was mocking the armies of Israel and God.

KEY VERSE: *David shouted in reply, "You come to me with a sword and spear. But I come to you in the name of the Lord of the armies of heaven and of Israel. I come in the name of the God whom you have defied." (1 Samuel 17:45)*

RELATED VERSES: *1 Samuel 17:12-58*

RELATED QUESTIONS: *Why did King Saul put heavy armor on David? Why wasn't David afraid of Goliath? How could David as a little boy fight a big, big giant? Why did the Philistines turn and run when David killed Goliath? How come David took Goliath's head with him?*

Q: WHY WAS SAUL JEALOUS OF DAVID?

151

A: After Saul made David an army commander, people were singing, "Saul has killed his thousands, and David his ten thousands!" (1 Samuel 18:7). It angered Saul that David had become so popular with the people; in fact, it seemed as though everyone liked David more than Saul. This made Saul jealous. Saul knew that David was a better man—a better warrior and a better person. This jealousy made Saul a very cruel and deceitful person, and he tried for years to kill David. Eventually God told Saul he couldn't be king anymore, and after Saul died, David became king. We must be careful to be content with whom God has made us and not become jealous of others.

KEY VERSES: *Of course, Saul was very angry. "What's this?" he said to himself. "They credit David with ten thousands and me with only thousands. Next they'll be making him their king!" So from that time on King Saul was jealous of David. (1 Samuel 18:8-9)*

RELATED VERSES: *1 Samuel 18:6-9*

RELATED QUESTIONS: *Why did Saul throw his spear at Jonathan? Why did an evil spirit come on Saul from God? Why would Saul want to kill David when he is married to his daughter Michal?*

Q: WHY DID SOLOMON WANT TO CUT THE BABY IN HALF?

152

A: After David died, his son Solomon became king. God told Solomon that he could have anything he asked for. Solomon asked for wisdom. One day two women came to King Solomon arguing over who was the real mother of a baby, and Solomon suggested that he cut the baby in half and give one half to each mother. Solomon didn't want to kill the baby. He just suggested that they cut the baby in half in order to find out who was the baby's real mother. Solomon knew that the real mother would never let such a thing happen to her baby. Solomon's trick worked, and the baby was given to his real mother. This story is in the Bible to show how wise Solomon was, in answer to his prayer. God made him the wisest man who ever lived.

KEY VERSES: *So [God] replied, "You did not ask for a long life. You did not ask for riches for yourself. You did not ask me to defeat your enemies. Instead, you asked for wisdom in ruling my people. Yes, I'll give you what you asked for! I will make you wiser than anyone else ever has been or will be!" (1 Kings 3:11-12)*

RELATED VERSES: *1 Kings 3:3-28*

RELATED QUESTIONS: *Why did God make Solomon rich when he only asked for wisdom? How did Solomon get to be so smart?*

Q: WERE PROPHETS THE PEOPLE IN BIBLE DAYS WHO MADE LOTS OF MONEY?

153

A:

It's easy to confuse words that sound alike but have different meanings. *Profit* refers to making money; *prophet* means a person who represented God to the people in Bible times. A prophet spoke God's messages and told the people to obey God. People never became prophets in order to become rich or famous. Most of the time—especially when they had to give bad news—prophets were very unpopular; some were even put in prison. But God's prophets were willing to risk everything for God. Some of the most famous prophets include Moses, Elijah, Elisha, Isaiah, Jeremiah, Ezekiel, and Daniel. Some less well-known prophets also wrote books of the Bible: Hosea, Joel, Amos, Obadiah, Jonah, and Malachi. Even though these prophets spoke hundreds of years ago, their messages apply to us, too, and we should listen to what they had to say.

KEY VERSE: *Long ago God spoke in many different ways to our fathers. He spoke through the prophets in visions, dreams, and even face to face. Little by little he told them about his plans. (Hebrews 1:1)*

RELATED VERSES: *Deuteronomy 18:15-22; Jeremiah 1:5; Ezekiel 2:5; 2 Peter 1:20-21*

RELATED QUESTIONS: *What does **prophet** mean? What does a prophet do?*

NOTE TO PARENTS: *Many children think prophets mainly foretold the future. But their main job was to "forth-tell" God's word to the people, to challenge the people to turn back to God. Often the prophets' messages contained predictions about the future, but most of the messages were calls or challenges to obey God and live right.*

OLD TESTAMENT EVENTS AND PEOPLE

Q: WHY DID ELIJAH GO UP TO HEAVEN SO EARLY?

154

A: Elijah was a famous prophet who spent most of his life telling others about God. He is one of only two people mentioned in the Bible who didn't die before going to heaven (Enoch is the other one—see Genesis 5:21-24). Instead, God took them. God used a chariot of fire and a whirlwind to take Elijah to heaven. The whirlwind and fire didn't kill Elijah or burn him; rather, the chariot and horses separated Elijah from his good friend and student, Elisha. Then the whirlwind carried Elijah to heaven. This showed that God approved of Elijah and that Elijah was a good man who loved God. And God took Elijah to heaven at just the right time, not early. We don't know how old Elijah was when God took him; he may have been an old man.

KEY VERSE: *[Elijah and Elisha] were walking along, talking. Then suddenly a chariot of fire came. It was pulled by horses of fire. It drove between them and separated them. Then Elijah was carried by a whirlwind into heaven. (2 Kings 2:11)*

RELATED VERSES: *2 Kings 2:1-12; Matthew 16:14; 17:3; 27:49; James 5:17*

RELATED QUESTIONS: *Why would God want to bring Elijah to heaven? Why was the chariot on fire?*

NOTE TO PARENTS: *Children often imagine that the chariot of fire would have killed Elijah and burned Elisha because it was on fire. We don't know what the "fire" was like. The point of the image is that God used a dramatic and miraculous event to separate Elijah and Elisha and to take Elijah to heaven.*

Q: WHY DID GOD SEND THE JEWS TO BABYLON?

155

A: The people of Judah (the Jews) didn't listen to the prophets. They turned away from God, worshiped idols, and mistreated the poor. So God allowed a wicked nation, Babylon, and a wicked king, Nebuchadnezzar, to capture their cities and take many of the people to Babylon. The Babylonians often did this to the people they conquered; they removed the best young people from their own country and trained them in Babylonian ways. Prophets like Jeremiah predicted that this would happen, and they were very sad about it. The Jews spent seventy years in Babylon, just as God said they would. God's warnings are for our good. When we ignore them again and again, we end up being hurt, just like the people of Judah did.

KEY VERSE: *King Nebuchadnezzar took 10,000 captives from Jerusalem. This included all the princes. It also included the best of the soldiers, craftsmen, and smiths. So only the poorest and least skilled people were left in the land. (2 Kings 24:14)*

RELATED VERSES: *2 Kings 20:17; 24:1–25:24; Jeremiah 34:1-22; Ezekiel 7:1-4; 8:17-18; 14:22*

RELATED QUESTIONS: *Why did God get a wicked king to take over Jerusalem and capture the people? Why did Jeremiah write a sad book?*

NOTE TO PARENTS: *The Babylonian captivity came as a result of Israel's failure to heed the prophets. It shows God's willingness to discipline his people for their own good. In Judah's case, the time in Babylon taught them not to worship idols anymore.*

Q: WHOSE HAND MADE THE WRITING ON THE WALL?

156

A: It was a miracle of God, performed to announce judgment on the king of Babylon for his pride. Belshazzar was holding a great feast and serving a lot of wine. During the eating and drinking, he sent for the gold and silver cups that had been taken from the temple in Jerusalem many years before by a king who ruled before him, King Nebuchadnezzar. As he was using these cups to drink a toast to idols of wood and stone, fingers of a man's hand appeared and began writing on the wall. The king was shocked and frightened, and he called for Daniel (one of God's prophets) to interpret the writing. It contained a message for the king: He had been evil and proud, and soon his enemies would defeat him (which they did). God used the hand and the writing to get the king's attention, and it certainly worked!

KEY VERSES: *They were drinking from these cups when suddenly they saw the fingers of a man's hand. The hand was writing on the plaster of the wall across from the lampstand. The king himself saw the fingers as they wrote. He was so afraid that his knees knocked together. His legs began to give way under him. (Daniel 5:5-6)*

RELATED VERSES: *Proverbs 18:12; Daniel 5:1-31*

RELATED QUESTION: *Why did God write on the wall?*

Q: HOW DID DANIEL SLEEP WITH THE LIONS WITHOUT BEING AFRAID?

157

A: Daniel was a young man when he was captured and taken to Babylon. He lived the rest of his life there, serving four kings, but he always remained true to God. One day, when he was an old man, the last of these kings, Darius, signed a law stating that no one could ask a favor of (or pray to) anyone except him, the king. (This was a trick by some powerful men to get rid of Daniel.) Because Daniel ignored the new law and continued to pray to God, the king had to punish him by putting him into a den of lions. Daniel spent all night with the lions but wasn't hurt.

The Bible doesn't say that Daniel wasn't afraid. Rather, Daniel was willing to face the lions because he trusted in God. Daniel had seen what God could do (see Daniel 3:1-30 and 5:1-31) and believed that obeying God was right, even if it meant being in danger. Even if Daniel was afraid, he faced the lions *bravely* because of his confidence in God.

KEY VERSE: *"My God has sent his angel. He shut the lions' mouths so that they can't touch me. I am innocent before God. And I have not done anything wrong to you." (Daniel 6:22)*

RELATED VERSES: *Psalms 3:6; 23:4; 27:1; 91:5; Daniel 6:1-28*

RELATED QUESTIONS: *Why did they want to throw Daniel in the lions' den? What would have happened if Daniel had obeyed Darius and didn't pray three times a day anymore?*

Q: WHY DIDN'T THE JEWS EVER CHANGE THEIR CLOTHES WHILE THEY WERE REBUILDING THE WALLS?

158

A: After seventy years in Babylon, God had the king begin to let his people go back home again. Although Nehemiah lived in Babylon and served the king there, he still loved his own country, Israel, especially the capital city, Jerusalem. When he heard that the walls were still torn down, he became very upset. (In those days, a city's walls helped protect it from invading armies, and good, solid walls showed that the city was doing well.) So Nehemiah asked for and received permission from the king to return to Jerusalem to organize the wall-building project. Not everyone in Jerusalem and the surrounding areas wanted the wall to be rebuilt; some were trying hard to stop the project. So all the workers had to be on guard constantly and to be organized so that the work could continue twenty-four hours a day. Nehemiah and the workers were so determined to rebuild the walls that they didn't change their clothes (except to wash) and always kept their weapons with them. Soon the wall was rebuilt.

KEY VERSE: *During this time we never took off our clothes except for washing. This included me, my brothers, the servants, and the guards who were with me. And we carried our weapons with us at all times. (Nehemiah 4:23)*

RELATED VERSES: *Nehemiah 1:1–2:20; 4:1-23*

RELATED QUESTIONS: *Why didn't all the Jews go back to Israel? Why did Nehemiah cry when he heard that the walls of Jerusalem were broken? Why didn't the Jews rebuild the walls of Jerusalem before Nehemiah came?*

Q: WHAT'S A MACCABEE?

159

A: The Maccabees were a courageous and heroic family of Jews who lived between the time of the Old and New Testaments. The events in the Old Testament ended about four hundred years before the events in the New Testament began. But during that time, Israel was still ruled by other nations, and most of the rulers were cruel to them. One ruler from Greece even made fun of the Jewish religion by sacrificing a pig in the temple. This greatly upset the Jews, and so they rebelled. The revolt was led by Judas Maccabee (who, by the way, was no relation to the Judas who betrayed Jesus). Under his leadership, the Jews were able to win many battles and eventually restore the temple to the way it was. They celebrated with a great festival, which came to be called Hanukkah, or the "Feast of Lights" (referred to as the "Feast of Dedication" in the New Testament). It became an annual event, beginning in December and lasting eight days.

KEY VERSE: *It was winter. Jesus was in Jerusalem for the Feast of Dedication. (John 10:22)*

RELATED QUESTIONS: *Why doesn't the Bible tell us about the four hundred years before the New Testament? What happened between the Old and New Testaments?*

NEW
TESTAMENT
EVENTS
AND
PEOPLE

Q: WHY WAS JESUS BORN IN A STINKY STABLE?

160

A:

God sent his own Son, Jesus, when the time was right. Jesus' birth tells us the kind of Savior he is. At the time Jesus was born, the Roman ruler of Palestine (where the Jews lived—Israel's Promised Land) was Herod, an evil man. Herod had great forts and palaces built so he could feel safe and powerful. One of the huge forts was right outside Bethlehem. But Jesus—the *true king* and ruler of the universe—came to earth and was born in a stinky stable. Herod's kingdom and power were very temporary; he's dead and his build- ings are in ruins. But Jesus' kingdom and power last forever. So one reason Jesus was born in such a place was to show us that he and his ways are the opposite of the world's. Jesus' kingdom doesn't come by force but by God working in each person. Jesus' birth in a stable also lets us know that he came for *all* people, not just the rich and famous.

KEY VERSES: *And while [Joseph and Mary] were there, the time came for her baby to be born. So she gave birth to her first child, a son. She wrapped him in a blanket and laid him in a manger. This was because there was no room for them in the village inn. (Luke 2:6-7)*

RELATED VERSES: *Luke 2:1-7, 11-12; Philippians 2:5-7*

RELATED QUESTIONS: *Did Mary have other babies, too? How could Mary have her baby without going to the hospital?*

NOTE TO PARENTS: *Children may ask the related question, "How could Mary have a baby if she wasn't married to God?" The best answer is, "I don't know." Exactly how Mary conceived is a mystery. Jesus was unique—the only Son of God. Jesus' birth was a miracle.*

Q: DID PEOPLE IN THE BIBLE HAVE CHRISTMAS?

161

A: Christmas is a celebration of the birth of Christ. Many years after Jesus was born, Christians decided to celebrate his birth. They chose December 25 as the day to observe it. December 25 is probably not the exact day Jesus was born, but that's not important. What is important is that we remember and celebrate the birth of Jesus, our Savior, not that we get presents, get time off from school, or get to eat a lot of sweets.

KEY VERSE: *Jesus was born in the town of Bethlehem, in Judea. He was born during the reign of King Herod. (Matthew 2:1)*

RELATED VERSES: *Isaiah 9:6-7; 16:5; Micah 5:2; Matthew 1:18–2:11; Luke 2:1-20*

RELATED QUESTIONS: *When was Christmas made? Was Jesus really born on Christmas? Why isn't Santa Claus in the Bible?*

NOTE TO PARENTS: *If your children ask about Santa Claus, explain that he was a person whom people have used to help celebrate Christmas. Many years ago, the real St. Nicholas was a man who helped poor children at Christmas time by giving them gifts. Since that time, the story has grown so that today we talk about Santa Claus, with his flying reindeer, who delivers presents to children all over the world. Santa isn't real, but Jesus is.*

Q: WHY DO ANGELS LIGHT UP AND GET BRIGHT?

162

A: When the angels came to tell about Jesus' birth, they glowed brightly. But angels don't always appear that way. When angels appeared to Abraham, for example, he thought they were ordinary men and offered them an evening meal (see Genesis 18:1-5). Angels may become bright to reflect God and his glory, or just whenever it is necessary, such as at night (which was when the angels appeared to the shepherds). As God's messengers, it's only fitting that they would light up and get bright because that's how it is in heaven, where they stand with God: "And the city has no need of sun or moon to light it. The glory of God and of the Lamb give it light" (Revelation 21:23).

KEY VERSE: *Suddenly an angel was there with them! And the hills shone bright with the glory of the Lord. They were very afraid. (Luke 2:9)*

RELATED VERSES: *Genesis 19:1; Exodus 3:2; Judges 13:6, 15, 20; Luke 1:11-20; 2:9-13*

RELATED QUESTION: *Why were shepherds afraid of angels?*

NOTE TO PARENTS: *People have many ideas about angels. Some think angels made regular appearances to biblical folks; in fact, they rarely did. Some think of angels as men with wings, yet many accounts don't mention wings. Some people speak of guardian angels, but the Bible describes angels as God's messengers, not our guardians. And some think too much of angels; Samson's parents tried to worship an angel and were told not to, and Hebrews 1 reminds us that Christ is superior to any angel. Your children may have different ideas about angels. Remember to look to God's Word for the truth.*

Q: HOW COME ZACHARIAS COULDN'T TALK UNTIL HIS SON WAS BORN?

163

A: Zacharias was a priest who served in the temple. One day he entered a part of the sanctuary where only the priest could go. There the angel Gabriel appeared to him and announced that Zacharias's wife, Elizabeth, would have a son. Zacharias doubted the angel's promise, and so he was silenced until the birth of the baby. This would be a sign to the people that Zacharias had met with God. When Zacharias's son was born, he asked for a writing tablet to write down the boy's name. As soon as he wrote, "His name is John!" as Gabriel had told him to do, Zacharias was able to talk again.

KEY VERSE: *When he finally came out, he couldn't speak to them. But they saw from his motions that he must have seen a vision in the Temple. (Luke 1:22)*

RELATED VERSES: *Luke 1:5-23, 57-63*

RELATED QUESTIONS: *What month was John the Baptist born? How come Zacharias asked for a writing tablet?*

Q: WHY DID JOHN THE BAPTIST LIVE IN THE DESERT?

164

A: John the Baptist was a prophet. God had given him the important job of preparing the way for Jesus. So John wanted to preach away from where people were living so they would have to go out to see him and hear his message. Living in the desert also kept him from having a lot of arguments with the religious leaders in Jerusalem who didn't like what he was saying. And by living in the desert, John was showing that he was serious about his message and that a person's relationship with God was much more important than having a nice, comfortable life on earth.

KEY VERSES: *While [Mary, Joseph, and Jesus] were living in Nazareth, John the Baptist began preaching in the Judean desert. He said, "Turn from your sins! Turn to God! For the Kingdom of Heaven is coming soon." (Matthew 3:1-2)*

RELATED VERSES: *Isaiah 40:3; Matthew 3:1-17; John 1:19-34*

RELATED QUESTION: *Why didn't Herod want to kill John the Baptist?*

Q: WHY DID THE HOLY SPIRIT COME DOWN ON JESUS LIKE A DOVE?

165

A: When Jesus was thirty years old, John the Baptist baptized him. When Jesus came up out of the water, the Holy Spirit came down on him in the form of a dove. The Holy Spirit is a spirit and doesn't have a body, so the Spirit took a form that people could see. A dove was a great form to take because when people saw doves, they thought of peace and purity, and that's exactly what the Holy Spirit brings to people. After Jesus left the earth, he sent the Holy Spirit to live here in his place. But now, instead of taking a special form, the Holy Spirit lives inside us. When a person trusts in Christ as Savior, the Holy Spirit comes to live inside him or her.

KEY VERSE: *The Holy Spirit settled upon [Jesus] in the form of a dove. And a voice from Heaven said, "You are my much-loved Son. Yes, you are my delight." (Luke 3:22)*

RELATED VERSES: *Matthew 3:16; Mark 1:10; John 1:32*

RELATED QUESTIONS: *What does the Holy Spirit look like? Where is the Holy Spirit today?*

Q: HOW DID JESUS DO MIRACLES?

166

A: Jesus was able to do miracles because he was God's Son. The miracles weren't magic or tricks; they really happened. Jesus performed miracles because he had compassion on people and because he wanted to show the people that he was the Messiah, the promised one from God. Only God can do real miracles. Sometimes God worked his miracles through special people, like the prophets or apostles. We read in the Bible about a lot of miracles, but miracles didn't happen every day. More miracles happened when Jesus was on earth than at any other time, but only during the three years that he was preaching and teaching in public. Jesus didn't do miracles to show off, and he didn't heal everybody. He had a purpose for everything he did.

KEY VERSES: *Jesus' disciples saw him do many other miracles besides the ones told about in this book. But these [miracles] are recorded so that you will believe that Jesus is the Messiah, the Son of God. And when you believe this truth, you will have life. (John 20:30-31)*

RELATED VERSES: *Matthew 11:4-5; John 7:21*

RELATED QUESTIONS: *How did Jesus get the coin into the fish's mouth? How could Jesus turn water into wine? Why did Jesus try to have Peter walk on the sea? How did Jesus make demons leave people? How could Jesus feed so many people with one boy's lunch?*

Q: ARE BEATITUDES SHORT FOR BAD ATTITUDES?

not so blessed are those with bad attitudes
not so blessed are those with bad attitudes
not so blessed are those with bad attitudes
not so blessed are those with bad attitudes
not so blessed are those with bad attit...
not so blessed are those with bad att...

167

A:

Jesus taught a short sermon called the Beatitudes to describe good attitudes, the attitudes that God wants us to have. The word *beatitude* means "blessed." Jesus said that whoever followed him should be poor in spirit, merciful, honest, and should expect rejection from others for being his follower. Jesus' disciples may have been thinking that they would become rich, famous, and powerful by following him, but Jesus was telling them that they should expect their rewards in heaven.

KEY VERSES: *One day, Jesus looked out and saw the crowds around him. So he went up the hillside with his disciples. He sat down and taught them there. (Matthew 5:1-2)*

RELATED VERSES: *Matthew 5:1-12*

RELATED QUESTION: *What was the most important thing that Jesus taught about?*

Q: IF JESUS DOESN'T WANT US TO GET HURT, WHY DID HE TELL US TO CHOP OUR HANDS OFF AND POKE OUR EYES OUT?

168

A: When Jesus spoke about cutting off a hand or poking out an eye, he was purposely exaggerating to make his point. This is called *hyperbole*. It's like saying, "I'd give *anything* to have an ice cream cone right now." Even though you wouldn't actually do *anything,* you want everyone to know how badly you want it. Jesus wanted to make people realize how bad sin is; it's so bad that you should get rid of *anything* that makes you sin. Jesus didn't want us actually to cut off our hands or poke out our eyes. Cutting off your hand won't get you to heaven and won't get rid of sin in your life. But saying it that way shows us how important it is to sacrifice habits, friendships, or attitudes that cause us to sin.

KEY VERSE: *"So if your hand or foot causes you to sin, cut it off and throw it away. It is better to enter Heaven crippled than to be in hell with both of your hands and feet."* (Matthew 18:8)

RELATED VERSES: *Matthew 5:29-30; 18:7-9*

NOTE TO PARENTS: *Jesus was also addressing the issue of legalism; the religious leaders were very concerned about keeping every letter of the law, and they had added hundreds of rules and regulations of their own. In effect, Jesus was saying that if they were serious about keeping the law, they should take drastic action. The point? Putting out an eye doesn't stop a child from envying his friend's bike; envy comes from the heart and involves the mind and imagination, not just what a person sees.*

Q: WHAT'S A PARABLE?

Good Samaritan
PAIR APPLE

169

A: A parable is a short story with a surprise ending that makes a point. Jesus told many parables for two reasons: (1) to hide the truth from people who weren't really interested, and (2) to teach the truth to listeners who were interested and wanted to learn. Whenever Jesus told parables, those who weren't interested or who didn't want to listen didn't understand. But those who wanted to learn asked Jesus to explain the story, and then they got the point. We can learn from the Bible if we want to do what God says. But if we don't want to listen to God, the Bible won't make much sense.

KEY VERSE: *[Jesus] used many such stories to teach the people. He taught them as much as they were ready to understand. (Mark 4:33)*

RELATED VERSES: *Ezekiel 17:2; Matthew 13:34; Mark 4:9, 30-34*

NOTE TO PARENTS: *Many younger children (preadolescents) may not fully understand parables. That's OK. Part of what makes parables powerful is that they can teach us more and more as we gain experience in life. Whenever you read a parable with your children, help them see how it teaches us to live. For example, the parable of the Good Samaritan is about a hurt man who receives help from an unlikely stranger after being bypassed by two religious leaders. Simply explain that Jesus wants us to be like the helper—compassionate toward others.*

Q: WHY DID THE DISCIPLES TELL THE PEOPLE JESUS WAS TOO BUSY TO SEE THE KIDS?

PRAYER ROOM

USHER

170

A: Many parents brought their children to see Jesus, and Jesus always welcomed them. The disciples tried to stop them because they didn't understand how much Jesus loved children and wanted all people to come to him. Sometimes adults act like kids aren't important or that children get in the way. But Jesus thinks kids are very important. He thinks *you* are important. Don't be afraid to bring your requests to him.

KEY VERSE: *But Jesus said, "Let the little children come to me. Don't stop them. For the Kingdom of Heaven belongs to such as these." (Matthew 19:14)*

RELATED VERSES: *Matthew 18:1-6; 19:13-15*

RELATED QUESTION: *Did Jesus talk to the kids?*

NOTE TO PARENTS: *Remember that Jesus told us to be like children in our belief in him. Watch your kids for clues about how this is done.*

Q: WHAT DOES PASSOVER MEAN?

171

A: Just before Jesus died, he had a Passover meal with his disciples. Passover is the special celebration Jews hold every year to remember when the Israelites left Egypt and started their trip to the Promised Land. Moses had told Pharaoh that because he wouldn't let the Jews go, all the firstborn boys would die. But God told the Jews to put the blood of a lamb over the door and on the sides of the door so the angel of death would see the blood and pass over them and spare the Jewish children. Today, Jews still celebrate Passover. Christians celebrate the Lord's Supper (Holy Communion) rather than Passover.

KEY VERSE: *"This yearly 'Feast of Unleavened Bread' will help you always remember today. It will remind you of the day when I brought you out of the land of Egypt. It is a law that you must celebrate this day every year, generation after generation." (Exodus 12:17)*

RELATED VERSES: *Exodus 12:1-30; Matthew 26:17-19, 26-29; 1 Corinthians 11:23-26*

RELATED QUESTIONS: *Why did they want to have the Last Supper in the house of someone they didn't know? Why did the disciples recline at the table to eat?*

NOTE TO PARENTS: *The Christian celebration of Communion comes from Jesus' celebration of Passover. Just before Jesus died, he had a Passover meal with his disciples. As they ate bread and wine, he told them that the bread was his body that would be broken for them and the wine was his blood that would be shed for them. Jesus is our Lamb that was killed; because of his blood, we can have eternal life.*

Q: WHY DID JUDAS BETRAY JESUS?

172

A: Judas turned against Jesus and betrayed him because Judas did not care about what Jesus had come to earth to do. Judas had hoped that Jesus would be a military leader and free the Jews from the Romans. Also, Judas loved money, and the religious leaders who wanted to kill Jesus offered Judas money to help them capture Jesus. If Judas had been one of Jesus' true disciples, he would not have betrayed him. Afterward, when he saw that Jesus was going to be killed, Judas was so upset at what he had done that he killed himself.

KEY VERSES: *Then Judas Iscariot went to the chief priests. Judas was one of the 12 apostles. He asked, "How much will you pay me to get Jesus into your hands?" They gave him 30 silver coins to do the job. From that time on, Judas watched for a chance to turn Jesus over to them. (Matthew 26:14-16)*

RELATED VERSES: *Matthew 26:47-50; John 6:70-71; 12:4-6; 13:26-30; 18:2-5*

RELATED QUESTION: *Why did Judas kill himself?*

Q: WHY WERE THE ROMAN SOLDIERS SO MEAN?

173

A:

The Roman soldiers were mean for the same reason that people are mean today—they didn't love God or care about his ways. Roman soldiers were trained to keep people in line and kill if they had to. The Roman soldiers were mean to Jesus because they treated all criminals that way and they thought Jesus was a criminal just like all the others. (Some religious leaders wanted Jesus crucified because they didn't like what he was saying and because he claimed to be the Son of God.) And the soldiers felt pressure from each other; one started and the others joined in. Though the Roman authorities found Jesus innocent, they went along with the crowd and killed him on the cross, just as the prophets had predicted (see Psalm 22:18; 34:20; Zechariah 12:10).

KEY VERSE: *[The Roman soldiers] beat him on the head with a cane and spat on him. They made fun of him by bowing down to "worship" him. (Mark 15:19)*

RELATED VERSES: *Matthew 27:1-37; Mark 15:1-32; Luke 23:34-37; John 19:1-37*

RELATED QUESTIONS: *Why did Pilate let Jesus be crucified when he knew that he didn't do anything wrong? Why did the bad men make a crown for Jesus? What does* **mocked** *mean? Why did they put a staff in Jesus' hand? Why did they cast lots to get Jesus' clothes? Why did they change Jesus' robe to a purple one?*

Q: WHY DID THE PEOPLE SAY, "COME DOWN OFF THE CROSS IF YOU ARE THE SON OF GOD"?

Gallery
Exhibit

174

A: The people who said this didn't believe in Jesus and thought he was lying when he claimed to be God. Actually, Jesus had the power to come down off the cross, but he didn't come down because he loved us and wanted to pay for our sins. When Adam and Eve sinned, everybody was separated from God. Jesus died so everyone could have the chance to be forgiven and be with God again. If Jesus had saved himself and had come off the cross, we couldn't be saved from our sins. Jesus showed his power in a much greater way—by rising from the dead three days later. Aren't you glad Jesus stayed on the cross?

KEY VERSES: *The people laughed at him as they walked by. They shook their heads in mockery. "Ha! Look at you now!" they yelled at him. "Sure, you can destroy the Temple and rebuild it in three days! If you're so wonderful, save yourself! Come down from the cross!" (Mark 15:29-30)*

RELATED VERSES: *Matthew 27:40; Luke 23:35-37*

RELATED QUESTIONS: *Why did they force Simon to carry the cross? Did they do the same thing to the two robbers that they did to Jesus? Why did people think that Jesus was calling Elijah from the cross?*

NOTE TO PARENTS: *A child's questions about Jesus' death on the cross may be a good opportunity to explain that he died for **them**, in **their** place, to pay for **their** sins. Explain that your children, individually, can trust in Jesus for salvation. You can lead them in a prayer confessing their sin, expressing trust in Jesus to save them, and thanking him for eternal life.*

NEW TESTAMENT EVENTS AND PEOPLE

Q: DID JESUS KNOW THAT HE WOULD COME TO LIFE AGAIN?

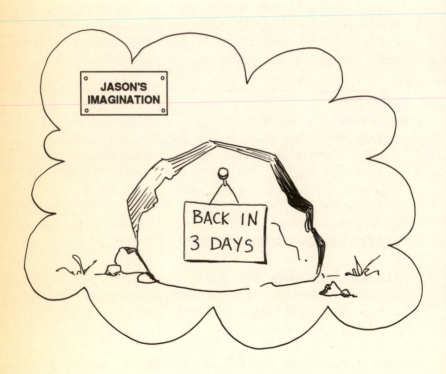

175

A: He sure did! He not only knew he would come to life again, he also told his disciples about it at least three times. But the disciples didn't seem to hear Jesus or understand what he was talking about because they were totally shocked by his death. They didn't expect Jesus to come back to life, so when they saw him, they didn't recognize him at first. But when Jesus came up close, talked with them, and ate with them, they knew it was him. After the Resurrection, Jesus appeared first to Mary Magdalene in the garden. Later, he appeared to two men walking on a road and then to the disciples gathered together in a room. He appeared to hundreds of others, too.

KEY VERSE: *"They will laugh at me and spit on me. They will beat me with their whips and kill me. But after three days I will come back to life again." (Mark 10:34)*

RELATED VERSES: *Matthew 16:21-23; 17:22-23; Mark 8:31-33; 9:30-32; 10:32-34; Luke 24:1-49; Acts 2:24; 1 Corinthians 15:3-8*

RELATED QUESTIONS: *How did the disciples recognize Jesus after he had risen from the dead? Who saw Jesus first after he came back to life?*

Q: WHY DID JESUS GO UP TO HEAVEN INSTEAD OF STAYING HERE ON EARTH?

176

A: Jesus is the Son of God, and his home is in heaven. He left his Father (and his home) to become a human being and live on the earth. So it's quite natural that Jesus would leave the earth and go back home. Jesus also went to heaven to prepare a place for us. And although Jesus left us, he also sent the Holy Spirit to take his place and be with us. Though Jesus couldn't be in two places at once, the Holy Spirit can; he can be everywhere because he lives inside all people who have trusted in Christ as Savior. Because Jesus went back to heaven, the Holy Spirit can be with you and in you, everywhere you go.

KEY VERSES: *"There are many homes in my Father's house. I am going to prepare a place for you. I will come again and take you to me. Then you will be with me where I am about to go. If this weren't so, I would tell you plainly." (John 14:2-3)*

RELATED VERSES: *Mark 16:19; Luke 24:50-51; John 14:1-7, 15-21, 25-26; 16:5-16; Acts 1:7-11*

RELATED QUESTIONS: *If Jesus is in heaven, does he still have scars on his hands, feet, and side? Why isn't Jesus here on earth now?*

Q: DIDN'T THE TONGUES OF FIRE ON THE APOSTLES' HEADS BURN THEM?

177

A: The tongues of fire that appeared on the heads of the disciples (after Jesus had gone back to heaven) symbolized the Holy Spirit who had come into their lives. The "tongues" weren't mouth-tongues, but tongues of fire. This "fire" wasn't real fire that burns things; it looked like fire, so that's how people described it. Everyone watching knew that something very special was happening. And when they listened, they heard their own language being spoken by people who hadn't learned the language. It was obvious that God was speaking through these people.

KEY VERSES: *Then, what looked like flames of fire settled on their heads. Everyone present was filled with the Holy Spirit. They began speaking in languages they didn't even know. For the Holy Spirit gave them the ability to do this. (Acts 2:3-4)*

RELATED VERSES: *Acts 2:1-13*

RELATED QUESTIONS: *When the Holy Spirit came on the people, why were there tongues of fire on their heads? How come the sound of a wind came when the Holy Spirit came?*

Q: HOW COULD THE ANGEL UNLOCK PETER OUT OF JAIL WITHOUT KEYS?

178

A: The angel freed Peter through God's power. Herod wanted to kill Peter to make some of the other leaders happy. He had Peter arrested and sentenced to death. The night before he was going to be killed, God sent an angel to rescue Peter. He woke Peter up, and the chains fell off Peter's wrists. Then Peter and the angel walked away from the soldiers without waking any of them up. God made the iron gate open up when they walked up to it. The angel left him when they got outside. Peter could hardly believe what had happened—and neither could his friends who were praying for him! (Acts 12:12-16)

KEY VERSES: *The night before he was to be killed, he was asleep. He was chained between two soldiers. And others were standing guard by the prison gate. But suddenly there was a light in the cell! And an Angel of the Lord stood beside Peter! The Angel slapped him on the side to wake him up. Then he said, "Quick! Get up!" And the chains fell off his wrists! (Acts 12:6-7)*

RELATED VERSES: *Psalm 68:6; Acts 5:12-29*

RELATED QUESTIONS: *Why did Peter go to jail? Why did the angel let Peter out of jail?*

Q: HOW BIG WERE THE WORMS THAT ATE KING HEROD?

179

A: King Herod had become very popular with many of the people because he had been hurting the Christians. Later, some people who were trying to get on his good side told him that he looked and sounded like a god. Already a very proud man, Herod enjoyed hearing what the people said, and he accepted their worship as though he really were a god. Because Herod did this instead of honoring God, God caused him to be filled with tiny worms, or maggots, that ate him from the inside out. In the Bible, worms are a sign of pain and punishment.

KEY VERSE: *Right then, an Angel of the Lord struck Herod with a sickness. Soon he was filled with maggots and died. This was because he let the people worship him instead of giving the glory to God. (Acts 12:23)*

RELATED VERSES: *Mark 9:48; Acts 12:1-4, 20-23*

Q: HOW COULD PETER KILL AND EAT ANIMALS THAT WERE IN A VISION?

180

A: Peter never actually ate the animals he saw in his vision; he received *permission* to eat them. You see, the animals Peter saw were the types that the Jews were not supposed to eat (called "unclean" animals). In his vision, a voice told Peter to kill and eat any of the animals he wished. Peter didn't actually eat the animals that he saw because they weren't real, but soon after seeing the vision, Peter learned its meaning. Three men who weren't Jews came to the door and asked Peter to come and talk to their leader, an officer in the Roman army. Normally Peter, a Jew, would not have anything to do with non-Jews (Gentiles) because they, like the animals, were considered unclean. But the vision made him realize that he should go with the men. Because Peter obeyed God and went with the men, the Roman soldier (Cornelius), his family, and his servants all became followers of Christ.

KEY VERSES: *In the sheet were all sorts of animals, snakes, and birds. Jews were not allowed to eat any of the things that were there. Then a voice said to him, "Go kill and eat any of them you wish." (Acts 10:12-13)*

RELATED VERSES: *Acts 10:9-48*

RELATED QUESTIONS: *Why did God make Peter have that dream? What is a trance? Why did God bring a sheet of animals down?*

Q: WHY WAS IT AGAINST THE LAW TO MAKE FRIENDS WITH A GENTILE?

181

A: A Gentile was anyone who was not a Jew. It *wasn't* against the law to make friends with a Gentile. Instead, God wanted the Jewish people not to copy and be like Gentiles because they didn't follow the Jewish laws and didn't worship the true God. Some Jews wouldn't even walk through Gentile towns. Jews did accept some Gentiles into their religion. They were called "God-fearers." By breaking down this barrier, the message about Jesus could be taken to everybody, not just Jews. God wants us to accept all people and not think we're superior just because we know God.

KEY VERSE: *Peter told them, "You all know about the Jewish laws. They say it is wrong for me to come into a Gentile home like this. But God has shown me in a vision that I should never think of anyone as impure." (Acts 10:28)*

RELATED VERSES: *John 4:9; Acts 10:1–11:30; Galatians 2:11-16*

RELATED QUESTION: *What is a Gentile?*

Q: WHY WAS SAUL BLINDED BY A BRIGHT LIGHT?

182

A:

At first, Saul (also known as Paul) was totally against Jesus and anyone who followed him. In fact, he watched and approved when a Christian named Stephen was killed for believing in Christ. Saul hated Christians so much that he got permission to capture them and put them in jail. But God had other plans for Saul's life. One day, while Saul was traveling to another city to look for Christians, he was blinded by a bright light. God used the light to get Saul's attention. Then Jesus appeared to him. Through this experience, Saul believed in Jesus. He became a strong follower of Christ and a great missionary. Instead of trying to get rid of Christians, he went all over the world helping people become Christians. He wrote many letters to those Christians; some of those letters are in our Bibles today.

KEY VERSES: *Saul was almost to Damascus to arrest the believers there. But suddenly a bright light from Heaven shone down on him! He fell to the ground. And he heard a voice saying to him, "Saul! Saul! Why are you trying to hurt me?" (Acts 9:3-4)*

RELATED VERSES: *Acts 7:59-60; 9:1-8; 26:1-18; Galatians 1:13-14*

RELATED QUESTION: *Which books of the Bible did Paul write?*

NOTE TO PARENTS: *Paul wrote Romans, 1 and 2 Corinthians, Galatians, Ephesians, Philippians, Colossians, 1 and 2 Thessalonians, 1 and 2 Timothy, Titus, and Philemon.*

Q: WHY DID PAUL WANT TO TELL THE ROMANS ABOUT JESUS?

183

A: Many people in Rome had become followers of Christ after visiting Jerusalem and hearing the message from the apostles there. Some had become Christians in other cities and had then moved to Rome. Paul wanted to meet these believers and encourage them in their faith. Rome was the most important city in the world at that time—the capital city of the Roman Empire. Paul knew that Christ's message had to go all over the world, and Rome would be a key place for helping to make that happen. Also, Paul was a Roman citizen, and he spoke Greek just as many people in Rome did, so he knew people would listen to him. Paul went on several trips all over the Roman Empire, including one to Rome, to tell people about Jesus.

KEY VERSE: *That night the Lord stood beside Paul. "Don't worry, Paul," he said. "You have told the people about me here in Jerusalem. In the same way, you must also be my witness in Rome." (Acts 23:11)*

RELATED VERSES: *Acts 4:27-30; 19:21; Romans 1:1–16:27*

RELATED QUESTION: *Does the book of Romans tell about the Romans who killed Jesus?*

Q: HOW DID PAUL SEND LETTERS TO CHURCHES IF THEY DIDN'T HAVE MAILBOXES?

184

A: In Paul's time, they didn't have a postal service like the one we have today. Instead, people sent letters by messengers or friends. Many of Paul's friends delivered his letters to churches. These friends included Timothy, Tychicus, and others. Paul wrote some letters, such as Philemon and Titus, to individuals. He wrote others, such as Romans and Philippians, to specific churches. And he wrote still others, such as Galatians and Colossians, to specific churches with the idea that the letters would be passed along to other churches. Paul's letters teach us about other parts of the Bible, about Jesus, about how Christians should live, and about how churches should be organized. Paul's letters have a lot to teach us!

KEY VERSE: *And remember why [the Lord] is waiting [to return]. He is giving us time to get his message of salvation out to others. Our wise and beloved brother Paul has talked about these things in his letters. (2 Peter 3:15)*

RELATED VERSES: *Galatians 6:11; Ephesians 6:21-22; Colossians 4:7-8; 2 Timothy 4:12-13; Titus 3:12; Philemon 1:12*

RELATED QUESTIONS: *If letters are only for the people they're written to, why do we read Paul's letters to other people? What did Paul say in his letters?*

Q: WHY HASN'T GOD TOLD US WHEN JESUS IS COMING BACK?

185

A: Jesus promised his disciples (and us) that he would return to earth some day. But when they asked *when,* he told them, "Such things are not for you to know" (Acts 1:7). Rather than be concerned with when Jesus will return, we should always live as though Jesus can return at any moment. In other words, we should always do what is right and tell others about God's salvation. Although God doesn't say exactly when Christ will return, he did say that certain things need to take place first. One of these is that Christ will not come back until the Gospel has been preached to the whole world. God has promised that Jesus will return soon and every day passed is a day closer to his return.

KEY VERSE: *"But no one knows the date and hour when the end will be. Not even the angels know this. No, not even God's Son knows this. Only the Father knows." (Matthew 24:36)*

RELATED VERSES: *Matthew 24:3–25:46; 1 Thessalonians 5:23; Hebrews 10:37; James 5:7*

RELATED QUESTIONS: *When is Jesus coming back? How come we can't see Jesus today?*

Q: IS THERE CHURCH IN HEAVEN?

186

A: In heaven, we won't have churches like the ones we have on earth because everyone in heaven will be a believer in Christ, and all of us will be together in God's presence. So we will be able to talk, laugh, pray, and have fun together all the time. We won't need church buildings either. We will see Jesus in person, so we will be able to worship him all the time, not just an hour a week. There will also be angels in heaven worshiping with us. We don't know exactly what worship will be like, but it won't include announcements, the offering, Bible reading, and a sermon. It will be pure joy. Think about it—we will be able to talk directly to Moses, David, Paul, and all the other faithful and famous servants of God!

KEY VERSE: *But we are looking forward to God's promise of new heavens and a new earth. Only goodness will be there. (2 Peter 3:13)*

RELATED VERSES: *1 John 3:2; Revelation 21:1-27*

RELATED QUESTIONS: *How big is the church in heaven, if there is one? Who gets to go to heaven? When we all go to heaven, will Jesus make something else on the earth?*

NOTE TO PARENTS: *Be careful of telling kids that in heaven we get to worship God all the time. They may think that they'll be singing hymn after hymn and listening to sermon after sermon for all eternity. Be sure to explain that heaven will be fun and exciting—better than Disney World, Nintendo, or any party they can imagine.*

Q: WILL I HAVE A BEDROOM UP IN HEAVEN?

187

A:

Jesus told his disciples that where his Father lived there were many homes. But we don't know exactly what that place or "house" will be like. In heaven, we will have what the Bible calls glorified bodies. In other words, our bodies will be different from what they are now. We will be able to recognize others, but we won't need food or sleep. We won't have bedrooms in heaven like the ones we have here; instead, we'll have very special places, each one prepared for us by Jesus. And we won't have to worry about the weather—the temperature will always be perfect. We won't even have to be concerned about what to wear—God will give us clothes. Heaven is a wonderful place, filled with joy, love, and happiness!

KEY VERSE: *"There are many homes in my Father's house. I am going to prepare a place for you." (John 14:2)*

RELATED VERSES: *John 14:2-4; Revelation 21:1-27*

RELATED QUESTIONS: *Will we live with our families in heaven? What do people walk on up in heaven, clouds? Will we see the twelve disciples in heaven? What kind of clothes do they have in heaven? Is it cold up in heaven? What is it like in heaven? Do people have birthdays in heaven and get older? Do people have babies up in heaven? Are there only old people in heaven?*

NOTE TO PARENTS: *Children always have questions about heaven. The questions listed above are good and indicate that they are thinking in terms of **things** and **personal security**. Let them know that heaven is a place of massive joy—they will like being there more than anywhere else. We don't know what will happen in heaven—only that it will be wonderful!*

BIBLE TIMES

Q: WHEN DID ALL THIS HAPPEN?

188

A: Everything in the Bible happened a long time ago—hundreds and hundreds of years before your grandparents were born. In fact, when you say what year it is right now, that tells about how many years have passed since Jesus lived on earth, and that's about when the New Testament was written. But many, many years also separate the Old Testament from the New. The events described in the Old Testament took place over thousands of years, and there are four hundred years between the last event in the Old Testament and the first event in the New. Although people who lived long ago didn't have TV, cars, computers, and other modern inventions, they weren't stupid. In fact, they were a lot like us. Those things just hadn't been invented yet.

KEY VERSE: *We were helpless sinners who had no use for God. Then Christ came at just the right time and died for us. (Romans 5:6)*

RELATED VERSES: *Genesis 1:1; Exodus 1:11; 12:40; Isaiah 54:9; Hebrews 1:1-2; 4:2*

RELATED QUESTIONS: *How long ago was the Bible written? Were people who lived in Bible times stupid?*

Q: HOW DID THE PEOPLE TRAVEL?

189

A: People in Bible times didn't have cars, trains, buses, or airplanes, but they still had to travel from town to town. Usually they walked. If you've ever taken a hike, you know that you walk until you're tired, and then you rest. You may even have to pitch a tent and camp out for the night before getting to your destination. Then you start hiking again the next day. That's what people did back then whenever they walked a long way. If they could afford it, people also rode on donkeys, camels, or horses. Sometimes people (usually kings, soldiers, or rich people) would ride in chariots that were pulled by horses. And, of course, when they had to travel over water, they went in boats or ships.

KEY VERSE: *"Eat it with your traveling clothes on, prepared for a long trip. Wear your walking shoes and carry your walking sticks in your hands. Eat it quickly. This observance shall be called the Lord's Passover." (Exodus 12:11)*

RELATED VERSES: *Exodus 12:34, 37-38; 13:20; 1 Samuel 25:18; Matthew 21:1-11; Acts 1:12*

RELATED QUESTION: *Did they have trains in the olden days when Jesus was down here?*

Q: DID CHILDREN IN BIBLE TIMES COLOR?

190

A: Children in Bible times didn't color with crayons like the ones we have today, but they did draw pictures. They also played games. Archaeologists (people who study ancient cities and cultures) have found some of the games. Children back then dressed differently from the way we do, their houses and schools were made differently, and they had different kinds of games. But they were just like kids today in many ways. They liked to have fun. They had family chores to do. When they were bad, their parents disciplined them. They studied. They had times of happiness and sadness. They were real kids.

KEY VERSE: *And the streets will be filled with boys and girls at play. (Zechariah 8:5)*

RELATED VERSES: *Matthew 11:16; Ephesians 6:1-4*

RELATED QUESTIONS: *What was life like for a child back then? Were there schools for Bible children to go to? Did Jesus go to school? Did they have sinners at school when Jesus was a boy? Did people in Bible times play games?*

Q: DO PEOPLE LIVE IN THE LAND OF ISRAEL TODAY?

191

A: Today, millions of people live in the lands where the Bible events took place, including Israel. Egypt, Iraq, Jordan, and Israel are some of the nations that now make up where Abraham, Isaac, Jacob, Joseph, Moses, Joshua, Gideon, Samuel, David, Solomon, Isaiah, Jonah, and Jesus lived. The cities that Paul visited are in parts of what we know today as Turkey, Greece, and Italy. Thousands of people go to these lands every year to visit places mentioned in the Bible. Some of the people there still dress much as they did in Bible times, but the big cities are very modern, with skyscrapers, telephones, fax machines, and computers.

KEY VERSE: *"I will never leave the people of Israel or David, my servant. I will never change the plan that his child will rule the descendants of Israel. Instead I will cause them to prosper once again. And I will have mercy on them." (Jeremiah 33:26)*

RELATED VERSES: *Jeremiah 33:24-26; Matthew 28:19-20*

RELATED QUESTIONS: *Can we go and see Babylon today? Do the people in Israel today worship God? Can we visit Bible people's homes? How come the Holy Land is filled with war and unhappiness?*

NOTE TO PARENTS: *If you can find a Bible map or atlas, show your kids where this all happened. Compare it to where you live. Tell them that Israel, Jordan, and other areas are called the "Holy Land" because that's where Bible events took place, but God isn't there more than anywhere else. Jesus told the disciples to take his message to the whole world, and we can serve God anywhere.*

Q: WHY DID PEOPLE IN BIBLE TIMES BOW DOWN TO WELCOME EACH OTHER?

192

A: In Bible times, people usually greeted each other with a hug or a kiss on the cheek. That's like a handshake today. They almost never bowed down unless they wanted to show humility, service, or great respect toward someone. People always bowed before a king or another important official. But when they were just meeting on the street or visiting one another's homes, they usually just hugged or kissed.

KEY VERSE: *Shake hands for me with all the brothers there. (1 Thessalonians 5:26)*

RELATED VERSES: *Exodus 11:8; 1 Samuel 25:23; Isaiah 60:14; Luke 24:5*

Q: WHY DID PEOPLE GO TO WELLS INSTEAD OF USING THE WATER AT HOME?

193

A: In Bible times, people went to rivers, streams, wells, and cisterns for their water because they didn't have indoor plumbing. (They also used candles and lanterns at night because they didn't have electricity.) A well was a hole dug deep into the ground to an underground spring. A cistern was a huge hole in the ground that collected rain water. Many people today use wells. Water from wells and cisterns is very clean. Although the people didn't have pipes and faucets, or chlorine and fluoride in their water like we have, they had plenty of good, clean water. And God gave them rules to follow that protected their health.

KEY VERSE: *"But you don't have a bucket," she said. "And this is a very deep well! Where would you get this living water?" (John 4:11)*

RELATED VERSES: *Genesis 24:45; 26:32; 37:24; Exodus 7:24; 1 Samuel 7:6; 2 Samuel 23:15-16*

RELATED QUESTIONS: *How did they light up their houses? Did the Bible people have electricity? Did Bible people have matches? How did people in the Bible make their candles? Did they have bathtubs like ours in Bible days?*

NOTE TO PARENTS: *Don't give the impression that this was crushing poverty. Due to the Old Testament laws, things were clean and sanitary.*

Q: DID PEOPLE HAVE SHOES IN BIBLE DAYS?

194

A: Because it is very sunny, hot, and dry in the Middle East (Bible lands), people usually wore sandals rather than shoes. Their sandals, made of leather, would be fastened to the feet with strips of leather attached to the bottom and wrapped up around the shins. Sandals protected their feet without making them hot. This also meant that their feet got dirty quite easily. Whenever people entered a home, they had to clean off the dust and dirt that had stuck to their sweaty feet. That's why Jesus spoke of washing others' feet as an act of service—it was a dirty job!

KEY VERSE: *Then [Jesus] poured water into a basin and began to wash the disciples' feet. He wiped them with the towel he had around him. (John 13:5)*

RELATED VERSES: *Deuteronomy 25:9-10; Ruth 4:7-8; Ezekiel 16:9-10; Matthew 10:14; Mark 6:11; Luke 7:44; 9:5; 10:11; John 13:5-15*

RELATED QUESTIONS: *How did people get their ears pierced in Bible days? Why didn't any people in the Bible wear glasses? Did anyone wear sunglasses in the Bible?*

Q: HOW COME THERE ARE NO BIBLE STORIES THAT TAKE PLACE IN WINTER?

195

A: Because the Bible doesn't mention snow very often, we might assume that none of the Bible stories took place in the winter. But, in fact, they took place at all times throughout the year. Bible lands are a bit too warm in the winter for snow, so that's why it's rarely mentioned. But it does rain in the winter. Though the winters aren't as cold as they are in the northern United States and Canada, there is snow on some of the mountains of Israel, especially in the northern area (where Lebanon is today).

KEY VERSE: *The snow never melts high up in the Lebanon mountains. The cold, flowing streams from the crags of Mount Hermon never run dry. (Jeremiah 18:14)*

RELATED VERSES: *Job 38:22; Psalm 51:7; Isaiah 55:10; 2 Timothy 4:21*

RELATED QUESTION: *Was there a lot of snow in Bible days in winter?*

Q: DID PEOPLE HAVE ICE CREAM IN BIBLE TIMES?

196

A: No. Ice cream was invented only about 200 years ago. But the Israelites had lots of good food to eat. Before God brought the Israelites out of slavery in Egypt, he promised Moses that he would give them "a land 'flowing with milk and honey'" (Exodus 3:8), and that's exactly what they got. Their land was very fertile, with rich soil for growing crops and grazing animals. The Hebrews had all kinds of delicious foods— figs, dates, honey, grapes, raisins, venison, bread, rice, lamb, milk, cheese, all kinds of vegetables, and other foods. They made cakes out of barley, raisins, and figs. Often they would flavor their food with salt and spices too, just as we do today. The Hebrews didn't have supermarkets, microwaves, or refrigerators, but they had plenty of healthy, delicious food.

KEY VERSE: *This was [the spies'] report: "We came to the land you sent us to see. It is indeed a wonderful country! It is a land 'flowing with milk and honey.' Here is some fruit we have brought as proof." (Numbers 13:27)*

RELATED VERSES: *Genesis 1:29; 2:16-17; 9:2-4; 27:3-4; Exodus 3:8; Numbers 13:23; 1 Samuel 25:18; 2 Samuel 17:29; 1 Kings 14:3; 1 Chronicles 12:40; Proverbs 25:16; Ezekiel 4:12; Daniel 1:12-16*

RELATED QUESTIONS: *What kind of food did the Hebrews eat? Was there pepper and salt in Bible days? Did the people before the Flood have different food than we have nowadays? Did people make cookies in Bible days?*

Q: HOW COME THE HUSBANDS COULD HAVE SO MANY WIVES?

197

A: Actually, very few husbands had more than one wife. Most had only one wife and lived with their families just as people do today. But some men, usually kings or rich men, would marry several women at once. A king might marry a princess from a neighboring country, for example, to ensure peace with that country. Other men married more than one wife because their first wives couldn't have children. No matter what the reason, God never wanted men to live this way. His plan is for a man to have one wife and for a woman to have one husband. Today people don't usually have more than one wife or husband (it's against the law), but they sometimes leave or divorce their spouses. But that's also not according to God's plan.

KEY VERSE: *This explains why a man leaves his father and mother. And it tells why he is joined to his wife in such a way that the two become one person. (Genesis 2:24)*

RELATED VERSES: *Deuteronomy 25:5; Matthew 19:3-6; Ephesians 5:31*

RELATED QUESTIONS: *Were families different or the same as ours? Did the fathers bring flowers to the wives in Bible days?*

Q: WHY DID PEOPLE KILL ANIMALS FOR CHURCH?

198

A: Before Jesus came, God's people had to sacrifice animals in worship to make payment for their sins. All of us sin against God, and that sin must be paid for. The animal took the person's place. (Not all sacrifices involved killing animals; some people would offer grain as a praise offering to God.) But when Jesus came, he died for every person's sin for all time. That's why John the Baptist called him "the Lamb of God who takes away the world's sin!" (John 1:29). The sacrifice of animals in Old Testament times represented Jesus' future death for us; the animals could not actually take away sins, as Jesus could (see Hebrews 10:4-7). Because Jesus died and rose again, we never have to sacrifice animals again. Instead, we worship and praise Jesus for all he's done for us.

KEY VERSE: *But Christ gave himself for our sins as one offering for all time. Then he sat down in the place of highest honor by God's right hand. (Hebrews 10:12)*

RELATED VERSES: *Genesis 4:4; Leviticus 17:3-5, 11; John 1:29; Hebrews 9:22; 10:1-18*

RELATED QUESTIONS: *Why did people worship idols in the Bible? How come idols were always cows and sheep? Why don't we have temples and palaces nowadays?*

NOTE TO PARENTS: *Kids are going to be repulsed at the idea of killing, but they would also be appalled if they found out where they get their hamburger, the details of which we hide from them. Actually, most of the meat sacrificed to God was given to the priests and Levites for food.*

Q: DID PEOPLE IN BIBLE TIMES HAVE MUSIC?

199

A: People had music in Bible times and loved it! Although they didn't have compact discs, tapes, pianos, or electric guitars, they did have many kinds of instruments. They also loved to sing. Singing praise to God was a very important part of their worship. They also sang songs to express their feelings. (All of the Psalms are songs—150 of them.) Often dirges (sad songs) would be sung when people were very sad. Perhaps the most well-known musician in the Bible is King David. He played the harp and wrote many songs, some of which are in the book of Psalms.

KEY VERSES: *Sing your praises to him! Sing with music from the harp. Let the cornets and trumpets shout! Make a joyful noise before the Lord, the King! (Psalm 98:5-6)*

RELATED VERSES: *Exodus 15:1-21; 1 Samuel 19:9; 2 Samuel 1:17-27; Psalm 57:7; 92:1; 98:1-9; 144:9, 150:3-5*

RELATED QUESTIONS: *If David wasn't a good songwriter would God still have asked him to write the Psalms? Were there pianos in the Bible days?*

Q: WERE THERE ANY CRIMES IN THE BIBLE?

200

A: Ever since Adam and Eve sinned against God, sin, and therefore crime, has been in the world. In fact, every person ever born has been born a sinner. That means that it is natural for boys, girls, men, and women to do wrong—to lie, cheat, steal, and hurt others. So crimes have been committed by people since the beginning. That's why we need Jesus. Only Jesus can take away our sin, teach us to do right, and help us love and respect one another. It all starts when we admit our sin, ask Jesus to forgive us, and invite him to rule our lives. If everyone did that and tried to obey God, there would be a lot less crime in the world!

KEY VERSE: *Meanwhile, the crime rate was rising rapidly across the earth. As seen by God, the world was rotten to the core. (Genesis 6:11)*

RELATED VERSES: *Genesis 6:1-11; 38:1-30; Matthew 6:19; Luke 23:38-43; 1 Corinthians 6:10*

RELATED QUESTIONS: *Were there any wars in the Bible days?*

Q: WHAT LANGUAGE DID THEY SPEAK IN BIBLE DAYS?

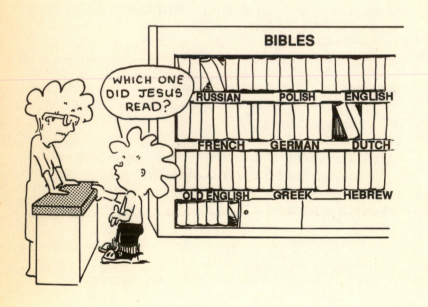

201

A:

At one time, everyone in the world spoke the same language. But they became proud and thought they were as good as God. When they tried to build a tower to heaven (the Tower of Babel), God gave them all different languages. That caused them to become confused, so they quit the project and scattered all over the earth. Ever since then, in Bible times just as today, each different group of people has spoken a different language. The most common languages the people of the Bible spoke were Hebrew, Aramaic, and Greek. In heaven, there will be people "from every nation" (Revelation 5:9).

KEY VERSES: *"How can this be?" they exclaimed. "For these men are all from Galilee. But we hear them speaking the languages of the lands where we were born!" (Acts 2:7-8)*

RELATED VERSES: *Genesis 11:1-9; 2 Kings 18:26-28; Ezra 4:7; Isaiah 19:18; 36:11-13; Daniel 2:4; John 19:17-20; Acts 2:6-11; 6:1; 9:29; 21:37-40; 22:2; 26:14; Revelation 9:11*

RELATED QUESTIONS: *What was the first language people had before God changed all of the languages? How come the people in the Bible have such weird names?*

Q: DOES GOD HAVE THINGS TO DO AT NIGHTTIME?

...PLEASE HELP US NOT HAVE TO WAKE UP
AT NIGHT, AND DON'T LET LOUD NOISES HAPPEN,
AND HELP THE CAT CATCH ALL THE MICE,
AND DON'T LET MY DAD SNORE SO LOUD
THAT HE WAKES UP MY MOM, AND HELP
OUR BRAINS TO KEEP ON WORKING EVEN
THOUGH WE HAVE THEM TURNED OFF, AND...

202

A: God does not have a body like ours, so he does not need to sleep. And because God is everywhere and lives in eternity, there's no night or day for him (and when it's night here, it's day somewhere else). So God is always working when we are sleeping. When you go to sleep, you can be sure that God is awake, watching over you and taking care of you.

KEY VERSES: *[God] will never let me stumble, slip, or fall. For he is always watching, never sleeping. (Psalm 121:3-4)*

RELATED VERSE: *1 Kings 18:27*